The Bible and Missions

The Bible and Missions

Helen Barrett Montgomery

with a new introduction by Sharyn Dowd

BAYLOR UNIVERSITY PRESS

Cover Design: Pamela Poll

Library of Congress Cataloging-in-Publication Data

Montgomery, Helen Barrett, 1861-1934.
The Bible and missions / Helen Barrett Montgomery ; with new introduction by Sharyn Dowd.
p. cm.
Originally published: West Medford, Mass. : Central Committee on the United Study of Foreign Missions, c1920.
Includes bibliographical references and index.
ISBN 978-1-60258-188-3 (pbk. : alk. paper)
1. Missions. 2. Bible--Publication and distribution. 3. Bible--Influence. I. Title.

BV2073.M6 2009
266--dc22

2008029716

Printed in the United States of America on acid-free paper.

This is the Book that "with authority"
Comforts, commands, both wounds and heals
the heart;
Not like a poem, or a history,
Nor yet like the flute and lute with all their art,
What lack I? do I tremble? weep? or frown?
Come, let me take this sovereign Bible down.

—Sarah N. Clegborn, in *American Magazine*—

Contents

Introduction

Sharyn Dowd

IN 1920 HELEN BARRETT MONTGOMERY published *The Bible and Missions* to celebrate the twentieth anniversary of the Central Committee on the United Study of Foreign Missions. At the age of forty-nine, she was at the height of her influence, both within the ecumenical women's missions movement and within her denomination, the Northern Baptist Convention. This new edition, with inclusive language for human beings, makes Montgomery's thought accessible to a generation of Baptist readers and students of missiology who are only vaguely familiar with Montgomery's work, if indeed they have heard of her at all. This edition is published by Baylor University Press a little over one hundred years after the appearance of Montgomery's first publication for the Central Committee, *Christus Redemptor: An Outline Study of the Island World of the Pacific* (1906).

Helen Barrett was born in 1861 to Amos Judson Barrett and Emily B. Barrows Barrett in Kingsville, Ohio. Her father was a graduate of the University of Rochester (New York) and her parents met when Judson Barrett was president of Nunda Institute, where Emily was a preceptress. In the 1870s Helen's father entered Rochester Theological Seminary, where he graduated in 1876. His only pastorate was at Lake Avenue Baptist Church, Rochester, which he served until his death in 1889.

Helen majored in classics at Wellesley College, graduating in 1884 when fewer than 2.2 percent of American women attended college. She taught in preparatory schools for three years before marrying William A. Montgomery, a business entrepreneur and member of the Lake Avenue Baptist Church in 1887.

Also in 1887 Helen Barrett Montgomery addressed a meeting of the Monroe Baptist Association, where she met her lifelong friend and co-worker in the cause of missions, Lucy Waterbury. Waterbury was the widow of a missionary; she later remarried and became Lucy Peabody, as she is known to historians of Baptist missions. Peabody is the author of the original Foreword to *The Bible and Missions.*

Montgomery worked in Rochester as a civic leader and member of the school board—the first woman to serve in that capacity. She became a well-known speaker in the city, addressing primarily women's groups on a variety of topics. She was an associate of Susan B. Anthony in the successful effort to have women admitted to the University of Rochester.

Always an active church member, Montgomery was licensed to preach by the Lake Avenue Baptist Church in 1898.[1] She and Lucy Peabody were among those who worked in the cause of ecumenical cooperation in the promotion and funding of foreign missions, a cause that received national attention in 1900 at the Ecumenical Missionary Conference held in New York City.

In 1910 Montgomery went on a national speaking tour as part of the "Jubilee" celebration of fifty years of organized women's work in missionary endeavors. She wrote a number of missions study books and edited a women's missions magazine. In 1921–1922 Montgomery served as president of the Northern Baptist Convention, guiding the convention through the crucial fundamentalist–modernist controversy, which resulted in the rejection by the Northern Baptists of a rigidly Calvinistic creed in favor of "no creed but the New Testament."

In 1924 Montgomery published a translation of the New Testament that she had originally prepared for her private use. This was called the *Centenary New Testament* because its publication commemorated the one hundredth

---

[1] The most comprehensive account of Montgomery's life to date is the dissertation of Kendal P. Mobley, "Helen Barrett Montgomery, 1861–1910: From Progressivism and Woman's Emancipation to Global Mission" (Th.D. diss., Boston University School of Theology, 2004). It is the source of the biographical material in this Introduction. Mobley's estimate that Montgomery's licensing must have been in 1898, rather than the traditional date of 1892 is accepted here.

anniversary of the American Baptist Publication Society.[2] Poor health resulted in her withdrawal from public life in 1930, and she died in 1934 at the age of seventy-three.

Helen Barrett Montgomery is known today primarily among the American Baptist churches in the U.S.A., the historical successor denomination to the Northern Baptist Convention. Among American Baptists her reputation is that of a proponent of foreign missions, the first woman to be elected president of a major American denomination, and (incorrectly) as the first woman to translate the New Testament from Greek into English. Among scholars of American and particularly Baptist church history, Montgomery's career is treated primarily by historians of the missions movement. But Helen Barrett Montgomery was also an assiduous student and teacher of the Bible; her Sunday school class at Lake Avenue Baptist Church included as many as two hundred and fifty women. In *The Bible and Missions* we see two of Montgomery's strongest interests presented in complementary fashion.

The Central Committee on the United Study of Foreign Missions was established in April 1900 at the historic Ecumenical Missionary Conference, headquartered in Carnegie Hall in New York City.[3] Montgomery attended as a representative of the Women's Baptist Foreign Missionary Society, which she later served as president from 1914 to 1924, with a hiatus of one year (1921–1922) when she was president of the denomination. Montgomery spoke twice at the conference. According to Kendal Mobley, her speech at Central Presbyterian Church on April 24

> was perhaps one of the most significant in the history of American mission theory, for it was the meeting at which the women's missionary boards announced their plan for united mission study—the plan that created the Central Committee on the United Study of Foreign Missions.[4] . . . Through its annual mission study texts, the Central

[2] On this see Sharyn Dowd, "Helen Barrett Montgomery's Centenary Translation of the New Testament: Characteristics and Influences," *Perspectives in Religious Studies* 19 (1992): 133–50, and idem, "The Ministry of Women in Montgomery's Centenary New Testament: The Evidence of the Autographs," *American Baptist Quarterly* 20 (2001): 320–28.

[3] Mobley, 374.

[4] Mobley, 375.

> Committee helped to shape women's understanding of missions, history, culture, and international relations for thirty-eight years.[5]

Of course there had been missions organizations and missions study materials for women long before Helen Barrett Montgomery and Lucy W. Peabody were born. It was not a shortage of study materials that the Central Committee found problematic, but the quality of the materials available. According to Montgomery, the literature that women received from the denominational mission boards was shallow and unchallenging. She referred to "little leaflets," given to the women "in homeopathic doses."[6] The Central Committee was sure that if women had study materials that stretched them intellectually and emphasized "that in this cause of foreign missions are included statecraft, and civilization, and geography, and history, and biography, and philosophy, and poetry, and art, and the living history of the living kingdom of God," interest and involvement would increase exponentially.[7] But it was clear that if the women wanted such study materials they would have to write the books themselves, which is precisely what the Central Committee set out to do. They would publish study books on missions written by women for women, not of a particular denomination, but encompassing the whole Protestant missionary movement.

The first year's study would be a history of missions "from apostolic times through the end of the eighteenth century." Though Harlan Page Beech, missions professor at Yale, advised the women that such a book would never sell, this first volume, *Via Christi* by Louise Manning Hodgkins, sold 50,000 copies.[8] Montgomery's 1910 book, *Western Women in Eastern Lands*, sold 100,000 copies and launched a "Jubilee" celebration of fifty years of organized missions work by women in the United States.[9]

The year 1920 was not only the twentieth anniversary of the Central Committee on the United Study of Foreign Missions, but it had also been

---

[5] Mobley, 376. Mobley cites, among others, Dana L. Robert, *Women in Mission: A Social History of Their Thought and Practice* (Macon, Ga.: Mercer University Press, 1997), 260–69, 274–77.

[6] Mobley, 377.

[7] Mobley, 377.

[8] Mobley, 378.

[9] Mobley, 387–88.

designated "Bible Year" by the Bible Societies of Great Britain and the United States. So when Montgomery was again called upon to write the celebratory volume, she titled it *The Bible and Missions.* This accounts for the organization and contents of the book, to which we now turn.

The Bible and Missions has two parts, the second slightly longer than the first. Part 1 has two chapters: chapter 1 begins with a general encomium on the topics, style, reticence, psychology, social passion, literary greatness, and theology of the Bible by contrast with other religions ancient and modern. The rest of the chapter is focused on a survey of "God's Plan of Salvation" laid out in the Law, the Historical Books, the Poetical Books, and the Prophets. Chapter 2 focuses on the New Testament as a mandate for and example of missionary activity.

Part 2 consists of four chapters. Chapter 3 is a history of Bible translation beginning with the Septuagint and ending with the achievements of the nineteenth century. Much of the material in this chapter is not part of seminary curricula in the twenty-first century, and is still an excellent summary for pastors and lay readers. Montgomery writes in an engaging style, covering in a few pages a wide range of important material, from the discovery of the so-called Nestorian tablet in northwestern China (1625), which recounts the arrival of Christian missionaries in China in the seventy century A.D., to an account of the fourth-century translation work of Ulfilas among the Goths to a series of stories accurately labeled, "Romances of Bible Translation." These deal with the adventures of translators like Carey of India, Judson of Burma, and Pilkington of Uganda.

Throughout the chapters the emphasis is on the forward march of the gospel into "heathenism" and "darkness"; if this cultural imperialism and religious triumphalism grate on the reader, let her consider that the very idea that women would be interested in reading about the history of translation had been incredible to the Yale professor of missions in 1900. It is remarkable that the advance of Christianity is celebrated without sectarian bias; Montgomery's heroes come from a variety of Christian confessional traditions. Unlike her evangelical successors, Montgomery did not treat Constantine's edict making Christianity the religion of his empire as "the fall of the church." On the contrary, one does not find anti-Catholic remarks until she begins to write about the later medieval period, and then the problem is not Catholicism per se but the fear of heresy that is blamed for the suppression of vernacular translations (88). In a subsequent chapter she makes one snide remark about the resistance of "the Pope" and some Eastern Orthodox leaders to the distribution of Bible translations, but does not dwell on the subject (117–18).

Having dealt with the history of translation, Montgomery turns in chapter 4 to the publication and distribution of Bible translations by the various Bible societies. This chapter includes a ten-page tribute to the colporters, or sales agents, of the Bible societies and closes with an exhortation to the reader to give financial support to the work of the Bible societies and to join the Pocket Testament League, pledging to carry a New Testament at all times and to read at least a chapter a day.

The topic of chapter 5 is the influence of the Bible on civilization. Here we see that despite the ravages of the Great War, Montgomery had not lost the optimism so characteristic of the Progressive Era in which she grew up and was educated. She writes: "Human society according to the Bible rests on no 'social contract,' but inheres in the plan of the Creator, who made [people] and nations to be members of one another in one great human family" (133). Her postmillennial zeal remains unshaken:

> No teaching is more needed today than the plain Bible doctrine that God has a will for the nations; that they are subject to his law, that those who break it will be punished as nations; that the Kingdom of God is no iridescent dream, but a great reality to be accomplished in this world through our cooperation with the God of nations in the upbuilding of human society. (134–35)

Montgomery's unconscious ethnocentrism is the most blatant in this chapter. She informs the reader that no non-Christian civilization has produced great music (138) and rejoices that in Uganda a "vast cathedral" has been built where "a vested choir discourses sweet music and great multitudes kneel in prayer" (141). She regards it as a triumph of Christian civilization that "Maori soldiers have been among the best troops which New Zealand sent to the front in France," remarking that "It is not three generations since their ancestors were naked savages" (142). Presumably, however, the uniformed Maori who died in the trenches of France were just as dead as their "naked" and "savage" ancestors who died in tribal warfare.

In 1920 it appeared to people like Montgomery that Japan and China were on the very brink of becoming part of the civilized Christian world: "A great sense of commonality is in the air. Converging from every nation [people] are walking on paths that lead to the Holy City coming down from God out of Heaven, and to that united humanity which has washed its robes and made them white in the blood of the Lamb" (152). But how could Montgomery and her contemporaries anticipate that the most unthinkable barbarisms in history still lay in the future: the extermination by German Christians of 6 million Jews and the obliteration by U.S. Christians of two entire Japanese cities full of noncombatants. Montgomery's naïveté is understandable; those who in the twenty-first century plot to visit the blessings of "the American way" on the "heathens" by force of arms have no such excuse.

The concluding sixth chapter emphasizes the positive effect of the translation and distribution of the Bible on the literature of both Western and non-Western cultures and the need for the publication of Christian literature in non-European languages. It is followed by "A Brief Reading List" of four pages and by an extensive index.

Although Montgomery stresses in the final chapter that Christian literature for Chinese women and children must not be "too bookish and intellectual," it is clear that the implied reader of *The Bible and Missions* is both well read and well educated. The reader is expected to recognize unattributed allusions to Kipling's "Recessional" and James Russell Lowell's "The Present Crisis," and to understand without translation a comment in French attributed to General Foch (commander-in-chief of the allied armies in WWI).

Her Christian progressivism is evident in a variety of passages: Montgomery assumes (and does not argue for) the division of Isaiah into preexilic and exilic sections, the recognition that the story of Jonah and "the whale" is to be understood as a "parable or allegory," and that the longer ending of Mark, from which she quotes "the Great Commission," is not found in the best manuscripts. She acknowledges two different interpretations of Malachi 1:11 and explains why the translation of George Adam Smith is better than that of the Authorized Version.

Montgomery writes for progressive Christians like herself; she refers to Charles Darwin as "the great naturalist" (143) and to Adolf von Harnack as "the great German critic" (84). She regards the philosophy of Borden P. Bowne, "in the ripest work of his mature thought, *Personalism,*" as a fine exposition of "the theistic conception of the universe," and rejoices in its translation into Japanese (25). In this assessment of the value of personalist philosophy for Christian social progress Montgomery was followed much later by her fellow Baptist, Dr. Martin Luther King Jr.

The twenty-first-century reader who is not a student of world history will need some help with Montgomery's many references to people and events much closer to her time than to ours. On page 37, the statement that "Judah was Assyria's Belgium" refers to the invasion of neutral Belgium by the armies of the Kaiser that so outraged the rest of Europe. Montgomery refers without explanation to Livingstone (David Livingstone, pioneer missionary to Africa) and to the Iron Duke (of Wellington), who defeated Napoleon at Waterloo in 1815 (68). The "great World War" is World War I (1914–1918). General Foch of France has already been mentioned. Montgomery also refers to (General George) Pershing, commander of American forces in Europe and a long list of other military heroes and politicians who would have been familiar and impressive to her readers in 1920, only two years after the Armistice.

This edition of *The Bible and Missions* is commended to pastors and to students of Christian missions for its sweeping grasp of the biblical storyline, its fascinating treatment of the history and methods of translation, and its emphasis on the important work of the (now Uunited) Bible societies. Perhaps most important for today's church is Montgomery's indictment of U.S. Christianity, which still stings as sharply as it must have done eighty-six years ago:

> [T]he Church has failed, up to the present moment, to interpret her own worldwide mission. She has spent her strength on definitions while the world lay in agony, has prated of "lesser folk without the law," while millions were denied their birthright in the gospel, has wrapped race prejudice about her like a garment, and from her coffers of abundance flung a few coins now and then, with which to finance the army of the Prince of Peace for the winning of the world. She has withheld hersons and daughters, denied her oath of allegiance, and all the while the Bible she professes to believe has been summoning her to abjure self and take up her cross of sacrifice and follow Jesus for the salvation of the world." (28)

Foreword

THE CENTRAL COMMITTEE on the United Study of Foreign Missions celebrates its twentieth anniversary by the publication of the textbook, *The Bible and Missions* by Helen Barrett Montgomery. In these days of reconstruction of Church and State, it is important that we come back to the authority in the Word of God for our great missionary enterprise. Plans of men, however wise, change with the changing years and with crises in history, but the plan of God is eternal. We rest our study this year on his own missionary message. The year 1920 has been appointed by Bible societies in Great Britain and America as Bible Year, which gives an added reason for a careful study of this subject and a wide effort to secure a more general use of the Bible throughout the world, especially in lands and among peoples who have never had the opportunity to read the Word of God.

The Committee is indebted to the American Bible Society for many of the unique and valuable illustrations in the book.*

Mrs. Henry W. Peabody, *Chairman*
Miss Olivia H. Lawrence
Mrs. Frank Mason Norht
Mrs. James A. Webb Jr.
Mrs. A. V. Pohlman
Miss Alice M. Kyle
Deaconess Herietta Goowin
Miss Grace T. Colburn, *Secretary*

* These illustrations are not included in the present edition.

Part I

Outline
Chapter 1

AIM: To show that the Bible is God's missionary textbook; that the missionary message, although most clearly revealed in the New Testament, is woven into the fabric of the Old Testament, and definitely proclaimed in its every part.

I. The Missionary Character of the Bible Seen in Its Essence and Substance
   1. Its topics, the great fundamentals of human thought
   2. Its style, uniquely adapted to translation
   3. Its reticence, the absence of crude cosmogonies that weigh down other religions
   4. Its psychology, a picture gallery of essential humanity
   5. Its social passion, humane legislation, and messages of the prophets
   6. Its literary greatness, impossible to exhaust or outgrow
   7. Its doctrine of God, the infinitely high, yet infinitely near

   All these and other qualities fit it to be the Book of humanity

II. The Missionary Character of the Bible is Seen in Its Positive Teachings

   God's plan of salvation, laid down in the Old Testament
   1. Missionary elements in the Law
      a. Its theism
      b. Unity of humankind

   c. Enlarging circles of blessing—Tragedy of Israel's failure to apprehend trusteeship
   d. Its prophetic note
   e. The Angel of the Presence
2. Missionary Elements in the Historic Books
   a. Discipline of the Chosen People
   b. Widening interests seen in Solomon's Prayer
   c. God's gracious calling of those without the Law
3. Missionary Message in the Poetical Books
   a. Poets the true seers and revealers of God's wider purposes
   b. Ruth and Job, illustrations of wider vision
   c. Psalms, the universal hymn book
   d. Particular messages of the Psalms—the heart of God, the messianic kingdom
   e. The Psalms in the life of Jesus
4. Missionary Message of the Prophets
   a. Missionary conceptions common to the prophets
      Israel, God's trustee for humanity
      Unity of human condition
      God's disciplinary providences
      The coming kingdom
   b. Missionary message of individual prophets
      Amos, God's righteous reign over all humankind; true religion spiritual
      Hosea, God loves his people
      Micah, Forecast of universal peace
      Isaiah, God's righteousness; providential government of the world; vision of the Suffering Servant and of redeemed humanity
      Jeremiah, his call; a type of Christ
      Ezekiel, the first gospel for the individual; the hireling shepherd; the healing waters
      Haggai and Zechariah, truth to go forth from Jerusalem; Messiah to speak peace to the heathen; his dominion to the ends of the earth

Habbakkuk, God's making the wrath of humankind to praise him, the glory of God to cover the Earth

Malachi, God's name revered among the heathen; the coming of the messenger

Daniel, the everlasting kingdom of the Son of Man

Joel, the outpouring of the Spirit

Jonah, God's thrusting forth his messengers; God's free grace over all his works

III. Summary of Ground Covered

One

The Missionary Message of the Old Testament

"That Book is not the book of a nation, but the Book of nations, because it places before us the fortunes of one nation as a symbol unto all the rest, because it connects the history of this one people with the origin of the world, and by a series of earthly and spiritual developments, of facts necessary and accidental continues it unto the remotest regions of the farthest eternities."

—*Goethe*

The missionaries: their Book

The missionaries have a Book which they take with them on all their wanderings; unless, in truth, it be the Book, which drives them forth on their great adventures. Certain it is that the biggest word for missions is the one spoken by the Book. Underneath all the smaller special appeals of the ages, of races and nations, of terrible sufferings of and appalling needs, is the great diapason of the Word—"Go ye; I am with you."

God's mission textbook

Reading the Bible meticulously for proof texts and argument, it is possible to escape its unmistakable drift; reading it in the large and simply as it was written, its missionary message is inescapable. For the church to recapture this great Word is to regain that "first, fine careless rapture" in which the early church set forth to win the world. If, leaving all little mission studies for a time, we could bend our minds and souls and strength to the study of God's mission study textbook, the world could no longer fetter the church.

Missionary character of the Bible twofold

The missionary character of the Bible is clearly seen in two great categories: (1) in its essential character; (2) in its expressed purpose and plan.

I. The Bible Missionary in Essence and Substance

The Bible is in its very subconscious subconsciousness missionary. Not only because of what it advocates or purposes or states, but because of what it is, the Bible is the great missionary charter of the church. Just as in measuring a person it is not so much their conscious words and deeds that count, but their very atmosphere and selfhood. The Bible being what it is cannot avoid becoming the Book of humanity. It is foreordained to universality.

Take its topics. They are the great fundamentals in which all men alike are concerned; life and death, sin and righteousness, God and the soul. It sets out to answer questions that rise in the soul of all people—savage and philosopher, saint and sinner, white and black alike, and will not be silenced. Whence am I? What does life mean? Where am I going? To what purpose is it all? Its answers have a quiet authority like the mountains, which do not ask our poor consenting.

Consider its style: so styleless that the Book can be translated into any language without loss of energy; so devoid of ornament that its poetry in all its naked beauty is poetry to Occident as to Orient; so free from all self-consciousness or pose that its narratives need depend on no adjective or descriptive phrase to heighten their effectiveness or drive home their point. Some of the most precious treasures of the world's literature are pale or tasteless in translation because their beauty is so largely in the marriage of thought to sound and rhythm. The Koreans say of the Bible, "It cannot be so beautiful in any other speech as in our Korean. It speaks to our souls." Of no other great literature can it be said that in translation it actually supplants the original in the world's esteem.

Great in its reticence the Book is adapted to a long life of continued influence. Consider the handicap which any sacred literature written in the world's childhood has to surmount; those impossible cosmogonies of the Egyptians, the Greeks, the Romans; that central mountain of Buddhism with its seven encircling ocean belts, each millions of miles in circumference; that Chinese view of the great Demiurge at work on his world:

> His breath made the wind, his voice the thunder; his left eye the sun, his right eye the moon; his legs and arms and fingers and toes into the four quarters of the earth; his blood into the rivers; his muscles into the strata of the earth; his flesh into the soil; his hair into the constellations; his skin and hair on it into plants and trees; his teeth and bones into the metals; the sweat of his body into rain, and the parasites upon him impregnated by the wind into the human species.
>
> *The Three Religions of China,*
> Soothill, *Page 177*

Over against these and all the other puerilities and coarsenesses with which the great ethnic Scriptures are weighed down, place the austere beauty of the first chapter of Genesis: "In the beginning God created the heavens and the earth."

The Bible has all the simplicity of the early ages. It does not attempt to express in scientific language what would have been incomprehensible for many centuries; but in what it does say there is a restrain, a reasonableness, a greatness, that enables it to hold its quiet way unashamed, while knowledge is increased in the earth. The students in India, Malaysia, China, or Japan who must study geography or astronomy or history, find their confidence in their sacred books undermined. In Christian lands the demolition of our false conceptions about the Bible under the impact of fresh knowledge, only serve to bring into fresh relief the unshaken Book. In its omissions, no less than in its statements, the Book shines by contrast.

In its psychology the Book is ageless. The heroes of ancient literature seem dwarfed by the centuries. Agamemnon, Aeneas, Beowulf lose their power to stir our imagination or our admiration. But about the life stories of the Bible there is a perennial, a universal charm. The men and women of the Bible are modern, ageless. In their temptation we trace our own; in their weaknesses and in their strength they are contemporary. With grave detachment the Bible sets them before us, glossing nothing, extenuating nothing, boasting nothing. "There they are, my men and women, bone of your bone, flesh of your flesh; look at them and ponder on the swift and solemn trust of life."

A picture of humanity

This psychology of the Bible seems never artificial. They are no puppets, but real folks, who react as we react under given stimuli. Hence their never-failing charm, their supply of sermonic material to fresh generations of sermonizers, their attraction to a ring of African faces lifted up by the flickering camp fire or to a college audience listening with delight as the foibles of Jacob, the supplanter, are subtly analyzed by some keen lecturer. Not least interesting on the great Bible canvas are those background faces, those individuals, those real persons whom you recognize in Paul's thumbnail sketches at the end of his letters. It is in this deep human interest that the Bible meets and vanquishes the greatest; so long as the most vital study for humanity is ourselves, the Bible's title to universal love is sure. It is full of personalities, deep and rich. It develops personality wherever it is read.

In its social passion the Bible stands forth supreme. In ages when the serf and the slave had no spokesperson, the Old Testament gave the laws from a God who cared. When women and children were still considered as "*impedimenta*" in the pilgrimage of the race, in the Bible a tender concern, a growing respect were visible. The prophets thundered for the poor in messages that are today tracts for the times, and in the New Testament the flowers of brotherhood bloomed in the world's darkness. No other sacred book even approaches the Bible in this concern for social values and social obligations.

The golden thought of the kingdom

The outstanding illustration of this social point of view is found in the thought of the kingdom of heaven that runs through the prophets. Whether they write to a nation established in its own land or to bondsmen scattered in captivity, the thought of the righteous rule of God among men increasingly dominates the prophets. They are social reformers with a vengeance. Across the centuries their denunciations still throb with passionate protest. "These men were so alive to God," says Rauschenbusch, "that they beat their naked hands against jagged injustice and inhumanity." The Bible alone of sacred books fervently cries aloud to a God of righteousness, whose will it is to set up justice in the earth. This one characteristic has made it instinctively feared and suppressed by all autocracies, religious and political, and beloved of the common people in every land.

The Bible is great literature. Big books make their way. They fly over seas, they tunnel the mountains, they bridge the centuries. By the common consent of humanity the Bible is supreme as literature. In its poetry of grandeur and of tenderness, in its sublimity and terror, in its tragedy and doom, in its lofty teachings and profound philosophy, in its story of the matchless life and words and deeds of Jesus of Nazareth, the Bible has a unique claim to be the Book of books, the Book of humanity.

In its presentation of the character of God lies the final claim of the Bible to universal interest. It is the conception of God which finally makes or breaks a person or nation, as people or nations tend to be conformed to the likeness of the being worshipped. The whole claim of the Bible to universal reverence might well be staked on this alone, the God whom it reveals.

The infinitely high is infinitely near

Beginning with the vague and inadequate ideas of God held by a primitive people, there is the steady education of the nation in the worship of one only God, infinite in power, awful in holiness, perfect in righteousness. Other books have enshrined great hymns to the Creator and have not unworthily sung of his power and glory; but in no other book is there found in such combination and such clearness the idea of an infinite Creator who summons to himself not only humanity's worship, but its reason; who upholds and forgives as well as judges; who demands justice as well as reverence, and whose awful purity calls for purity of life and purpose in his worshippers.

Failure of ethnic faiths in their doctrine of God

The Hindus have seen God's immanence, but not his transcendence, how he is *in* but not *over* his universe, and so have lost themselves in the fogs of pantheism. Failing to perceive his unity, the Greek, the Roman, the Egyptian, and the Indian faiths sank into the debasing superstitions of idolatry. In all literature there is not more biting satire than is poured upon the idolater in Isaiah and the Psalms (Isa 40; Ps 115).

God's holiness and God's goodness

The clear teaching in regard to the holiness of God has made impossible the divorce between religion and ethics wherever the Bible is adequately taught or obeyed. The thought of God's holiness is supplemented by that loftiest and sweetest thought of God, clearly revealed in Jesus Christ, his fatherly love and compassion. God is light! God is love! The Book that reveals such a God cannot be kept from becoming the Book of the race.

The Book begins its journeyings

In point of fact, the essential character of the Old Testament Scriptures was actually in process of beginning the Bible's missionary pilgrimage years before the coming of Christ, when the Septuagint translation into the Greek language was made. This is the first instance in history in which the sacred books of one nation were translated into another language, and in translation far outstripped the original in circulation and influence.

II. The Bible is missionary in its positive teachings

While the message of the Bible to humankind is thus presupposed in its essential nature and character, we are not left without the most clear and positive missionary teachings. These are found in germ in the Old Testament and are fully developed in the New. This is what we should expect, as the Old Testament finds its completion and justification in the New. What is not so clearly evident regarding the plan while the foundation is being laid and the walls are rising, is evident when the complete structure is inspected.

God's plan of the ages

Jesus himself rejoiced in spirit as the deep things of God dawned on men in the springtime of the coming kingdom. "I thank thee, Father," he cried, "that thou hast hidden these things from the wise and prudent, and revealed them unto babes." There is a sense of rapture in the letters of Paul, as he contemplates God's plan of the Ages now so clearly seen in Christ. For there is a plan, although the phrase "plan of salvation," so popular in times past, is now seldom heard. The trouble is not with the phrase or the idea behind it, but with its misapplication and misuse. We do not send out missionaries to proclaim a "plan of salvation," but Christ and the power of his resurrection. We are not saved by a "plan," but by a person. We do not exhibit the working drawings of our house; we show our friends through our home; nevertheless the architect had a plan and the builder followed it.

John and Paul see the plan

So there is an august plan of salvation on which all Scripture is built together for an habitation of the spirit of humanity. John catches a gleam of the vast design when he speaks of the Lamb slain from the foundation of the world. Paul's great intellect is incandescent as the glory of God's purpose dawns upon him. Human language bends and breaks under the weight of glory with which he loads it as he tries to put into words, in the opening chapter of his letter to the Ephesians, his vision of the plan.

> "For this reason," so he begins in the third chapter to sum up the mighty argument of the first and second chapters, "I, Paul, the pris-

oner of Christ Jesus on behalf of you Gentiles, for surely you have heard of the stewardship of the grace of God entrusted to me for you; and how by direct revelation the secret truth was made known to me, as I have already briefly written to you, by reading which you can judge of my insight into that secret truth of Christ which was not made plain to the sons of men in former generations as it has now been revealed by the Spirit to his holy apostles and prophets, namely, that in Christ Jesus the heathen are one body with us and are co-heirs and co-partners in the promises through the gospel. It is of this gospel I became a minister according to the gift of the grace of God bestowed upon me by the energy of his power."

"To me who am less than the least of all saints has this grace been given, that I should proclaim among the heathen the gospel of the unsearchable riches of Christ, and should make all men see the new dispensation of that secret purpose hidden from eternity in the God who founded the universe in order that now God's manifold wisdom should, through the church, be made known to the principalities and powers in the heavenly sphere, according to his eternal purpose which he purposed in Christ Jesus our Lord, in whom we have boldness and access in the confidence of his faith."

The scarlet thread of Scripture

This plan of God so clearly to be traced throughout the Scripture is indeed a mystery. Here are writings separated by centuries, composed under circumstances the most diverse, written by men of varied gifts and capacities, yet all so assembled about one master idea that no sense of violence is felt when all are gathered together in one volume and called "the Book." There is no such underlying unity discernible in any other sacred writing; not in the Koran, written by the one prophet Mahomet; not in the multitudinous and contradictory scriptures of Hinduism; not in the Hina-Yana and Maha-Yana of Buddhism. Paul did not invent the plan; he discovered it.

The Bible, the record of God's search for humanity

To sketch a plan so vast in a few words is well nigh impossible; but even if inadequate it is still true to say that the Bible records God's search for humanity for the purpose of redemption and fellowship with himself. Other sacred books record the story of humanity's search for God. The Bible reverses the process. From first to last it is Christocentric. In the Old

Testament may be traced the first working drawings of the plan; the promise in the garden; the training of the family and people chosen to bless all nations; the messages through the prophets; the promises of the Messiah; in its completion and fulfillment in the New Testament, by which the dimness and misunderstandings of the past are done away in the light of the glory God revealed in the face of Jesus Christ, God is seen fighting for humanity, to redeem them himself into sonship.

Unfolding of plan in Old Testament

It will be convenient to consider first the plan of God for the salvation of the world as it unfolds throughout the Old Testament under the four divisions into which the Hebrews divided their sacred writings—the Law, the History, the Prophets, the Writings—and then to take up the missionary teachings of the New Testament.

(1) Missionary message in the Law

The Law, that is the Pentateuch, the five books of Moses, was *the* Bible of Judaism. To it all other parts of the Scriptures were supplementary or subordinate. It was the Law to whose expounding the Rabbis gave their study, day and night. It was this venerable code out of which they formed a yoke intolerable to be borne because of its subtleties, its puerilities, its multitudinous legislations on the minutiae of human conduct. Yet it was the Law, out of whose inferences Scribes and Pharisees had created an instrument of oppressive formalism and into which they had read their own bitter intolerance and nationalism, that the author of the Hebrews recognized as the shadow of better things to come, "a living book, rich in vital growth and in symbolic anticipations, a long, fibrous root out of which came the new law of the Mount and a greater prophet like unto Moses."

The Pentateuch's revelation of God and his plan

The Pentateuch plants itself squarely on theism, and that in itself is a fundamental missionary message. The main conception, out of which sprang Christianity's most precious and distinctive thought of God, is planted in Genesis, and overshadows the Pentateuch. "God," "I Am," "Jehovah," the righteous Ruler and Creator, is seen to have a purpose for his world of humankind.

(a) God, the great person

A great deal of shallow criticism has been passed upon the old Bible for what has been called its "anthropomorphism"—its God in the likeness of men. But through whatever naïveté and childlikeness of statement the idea had to find its way, it is becoming increasingly evident that the theistic conception of the universe is today Christianity's final challenge to blank materialism. Since personality is our own final perception of reality, we must begin to interpret the ultimate reality in terms of the highest power within the circle of our own experience. Step by step the revelation of an orderly and rational universe has kept pace with our experience of God, until today multitudes of every race find the meaning to existence in the God and Father of our Lord Jesus Christ, who of old time became the God of Abraham, of Isaac, and of Jacob.

Personalism *translated into Japanese*

Professor Borden P. Bowne, in the ripest work of his mature thought, *Personalism*, has magnificently expounded the philosophy to which the theistic conception of the universe, implicit in the ancient book of the Law, inevitably leads—"A world of persons with a Supreme Person at the head." His book has been felt to be of such value to the thought of Japan that it has been translated by a committee made up of American and Japanese scholars and published, after being subjected to the criticism of the classroom in the Doshisha University for three years. The reception of the book has shown that Japan is keen for this thorough-going philosophical interpretation of Christian theism.

(b) Humankind, of one blood

The missionary message of the Law is found also in its story of the origin of humanity; "And God said, Let us make people in our own image," declared the Old Law. Anthropology, philology, archaeology, and biology unite today to reinforce that sublime declaration. Every added bit of knowledge makes clearer the truth so long derided and denied, and so long affirmed by God's Holy Word, that humankind is one._In spite of confusion of tongues and deep social cleavages; in spite of differences in color and customs that merely point to deeper divergencies of thought and ideal, the ancient Scripture stands. Paul's bold declaration, so opposed to the belief of the educated Greek or Roman of his day, is today a foundation affirmation of science.

> He caused to spring from one forefather people of every race, for them to live on the whole surface of the earth, and marked out for them an appointed span of life and the boundaries of their homes; that they might seek God, if perhaps they could grope for him and find him.
>
> *Acts 17:26-27 (Weymouth)*

(c) The enlarging circles of blessing

The missionary message of the Law is found, too, in its story of the choice of a person, a family, a nation, to be Jehovah's servant for the world. Back of the choice is always the purpose to bless. "And in thy seed shall all the nations of the earth be blessed."

A channel of blessing, not a pool of privilege

This purpose of election, to be a channel of blessing, is repeated to Jacob and reasserted to each of the patriarchs. (Gen 12;1-3; 17:18; 22:18; 26:4; 28:14). In Jacob's wonderful blessings to his sons, the old man rises to the height of pure prophetic universalism:

> The scepter shall not depart from Judah,
> Nor the ruler's staff from between his feet,
> Until Shiloh come (He come whose it is—Syriac);
> And unto him shall the obedience of the peoples be.
>
> *Genesis 49:10*

Israel, trustee for humanity

In the picture of Exodus 19:3-6, the new-born nation looks back across the Red Sea to its days of bondage and forward to the land of promise. At this solemn moment Moses received from the hand of God the nation's commission, as Jehovah spoke to him from the burning mountain.

> Thus shalt thou say to the house of Jacob, and tell the children of Israel: Ye have seen what I did unto the Egyptians, and how I bare you on eagles' wings, and brought you unto myself. Now therefore, if ye will obey my voice indeed, and keep my covenant, then ye shall be mine own possession from among all peoples: for all the earth is mine: and ye shall be unto me a kingdom of priests and a holy nation.

Says Carver:

> First let Israel get her bearings. First let the people learn the reason for their separate existence. Let them hear the meaning of their past preservation and their future career. It was God who had acted on them and on the Egyptians. He had brought the children of Israel, not to Canaan, not to glory, but "to himself." Now their future as peculiarly his own people will depend upon their obeying genuinely his voice

and keeping his convenant—covenant inherited through Abraham and to be made anew with the nation. Such was his character and such his plan with Israel that only thus could he afford to make them his special own, above all peoples, as they reflected his glory among men. They must not forget that all the earth is his and all its peoples. If he takes this one tribe to his heart for the time it is not to forget the rest, but to do good to all. His aim is that Israel shall serve him as a kingdom of priests, a nation set apart to prophetic service. But when the priest and the prophet are a nation, the people for whom they minister and to whom they prophesy are the other nations. Abraham's call lies at the basis of Israel's election in the plan of God.

Israel transmutes election into privilege

The central sin of Israel was its failure to discern the meaning of God's election of his servant nation. What God meant for all humankind, Israel monopolized.

> "A light to lighten the Gentiles, and the glory of thy people, Israel,"

was the vision of Simeon's enlightened heart.

> "I will give thee for a light to the Gentiles, that thou mayest be my salvation to the end of the earth,"

sang Isaiah. But the mind of the nation stuck on privilege, and its eyes were jealously bent earthward or haughtily averted from other nations. The election to service was transmuted into a charter of privilege. Pride in their distinctive calling became the ground of the narrowest exclusiveness. The nation chosen to be the servant of Jehovah turned Pharisee, thanking God that it was not as other nations, and perished behind the hedge of a law interpreted to exclude all Gentiles from the promises of Jehovah. The nation turned from the worldwide vision of the prophets to the disputations of warring sects, and, though custodians of the ideal kingdom of God on earth, failed to recognize the king when he came.

The tragedy of Israel's failure

It is one of the tragedies of history, this failure of the Jewish nation to perform the service for which it had been chosen and set apart by God. A mystery, too, when all the time the Jews possessed the antidote to their fatal narrowness of vision in their own Scriptures. It was the vision of this tragedy over which Jesus wept as he looked upon the Holy City from the brow of the Mount of Olives.

Other lights that failed

Let us not be too hard upon the Jews. Theirs is not the only instance of a nation richly dowered for service that failed God. The Jews, set apart to witness to the one true living God to all the earth, failed, and their candlestick was removed out of its place. The Greeks, more richly gifted than any other race to spread the light of art and culture among the nations, looked with haughty scorn upon all outside "barbarians," dimmed the light of their radiant souls by unworthy pleasures, and their candlestick, too, was removed. The Romans, magnificently equipped to organize the world in one great system of law and justice, fell to worshipping brute force and cruelty, and their light also failed.

Will the Christian church fail?

Will the Christian church prove another tragic instance of a thwarted purpose of God? Walking not by the flickering torch of the Old Testament, but in the full blaze of light that streams from the cross of Christ, inheriting his promises, his commands, his love for the whole wide world, the church has failed, up to the present moment, to interpret her own worldwide mission. She has spent her strength on definitions while the world lay in agony, has prated of "lesser folk without the law," while millions were denied their birthright in the gospel, has wrapped race prejudice about her like a garment, and from her coffers of abundance flung a few coins now and then, with which to finance the army of the Prince of Peace for the winning of the world. She has withheld her sons and daughters, denied her oath of allegiance, and all the while the Bible she professes to believe has been summoning her to abjure self and take up her cross of sacrifice and follow Jesus for the salvation of the world.

The gospel will not fail

The gospel will not fail. The Lord Jesus shall see of the travail of his soul and be satisfied. The kingdoms of this world shall become the kingdom of our Lord and of his Christ. *But the church may fail*, may be set aside for another instrument. Today is the day of salvation for our Protestant churches. If we harden our hearts and close our eyes and refuse the plain call of God, other generations may see in us another Israel whose narrowness of vision was condemned by the very Scripture in which is our boast.

(d) In the prophetic note

The missionary message of the law is found in its prophetic note. Running through the book of Genesis like the first faint streaks of dawn are premonitions of universalism. The first promise of redemption is made to the mother of all living (Gen 3:15) in the person of that mysterious seed who shall bruise the serpent's head. In Melchizadek, King of Salem, priest of the Most High God, there rises a majestic figure out of the shadowy unknown peoples. To him Abraham, the father of the chosen people, pays tithes as an inferior to a superior, recognizing in him a messenger of the Most High God, possessor of heaven and earth. The author of the letter to the Hebrews uses this incident at length to bring to the consciousness of Hebrew converts that wider priesthood which took its origin, not from the ritual of human legislation, but was made in the power of that Endless Life which enlightens everyone born into the world, Jew or Gentile (Heb 7:1-16).

(e) The angel of the presence

The mysterious angel of the Lord, recognized with such awe and trembling as the dread presence of divinity, comes and goes through the story, the first faint revelation of Immanuel, God with us, the glory and the heart of the Christian message. See Gen 16:7, 22:11-15, 32:24-30, 35:9-13; Exod 3:2-6, 14:19, 23:20-23; Num 22:31; Josh 5:13-15.

(2) Missionary message of the historical books

The missionary meaning of the so-called "historical books" that follow the Pentateuch is not so clear as that of the Law. If the theories of the modern school of interpreters are correct, these are for the most part earlier writings in which the missionary understanding of Israel's mission is naturally less clear. Under any interpretation the life story of the Hebrew people is profitable for instruction in righteousness. The long discipline of the people culminating in the captivity sees Israel at last weaned from his idols and devoted in his soul to the worship of the one true God. It is interesting to note that the two other religions that are uncompromisingly monotheistic, Islam and Christianity, spring from Judaism. In these long centuries of disaster and apostasy the hope of a coming King beams constantly clearer.

The foreigner in Solomon's prayer of dedication

One of the outstanding instances of a wider than national meaning in the story is found in 1 Kings 5, where Hiram, king of Tyre, congratulates Solomon on his purpose to build a temple for God, furnishes him with great cedars of Lebanon, and the two kings cement one of the earliest "leagues of nations." In Solomon's prayer of dedication that follows, we catch solemn overtones of the universal gospel.

> Moreover concerning the foreigner, that is not of thy people Israel, when he shall come out of a far country for my name's sake (for they shall hear of thy great name, and of thy mighty hand, and of thine outstretched arm); when he shall come and pray toward this house; hear thou in heaven thy dwelling-place, and do according to all that the foreigner calleth to thee for; that all the peoples of the earth may know thy name, to fear thee, as doth thy people Israel, and that they may know that this house which I have built is called by thy name.
>
> *1 Kings 8:41-43*

God's gracious calling outside the Law

Our Lord was quick to call the attention of the orthodox Jews of his day to God's gracious care for his children outside of the pale of the chosen people. "I tell you truly," he said, "that in Israel there were many widows during the days of Elijah, when the sky was closed for three years and six months, when a great famine came over all the land; yet Elijah was not sent to any of these, but only to a widow woman at Zarephath in Sidon; and in Israel there were many lepers in the time of the prophet Elisha, yet none of them was cleansed, but only Naaman the Syrian" (Luke 4:25-27).

Resented by the orthodox

So violent are human prejudices, so slow of heart are people to believe and rejoice in the wide plans of God, who is no respecter of persons, that the effect of this gracious unfolding of the wider applications of their own Scriptures was that "all in the synagogue were filled with rage and rose up and put him out of the town and brought him to the brow of the hill on which their town was built, in order to hurl him down."

The captive Syrian maid

Still another exquisite missionary pendant is the story of the captive maid in the house of Naaman the leper, whose heart goes out quite naturally and simply in the desire to share God's grace with those who know it not, humble protagonist of those thousands who today in far distant lands are telling of the great fountain which God has opened for the cleansing of human sin (2 Kgs 5:2-3).

(3) Missionary message in the poetical books

The poets are ever the "makers," the "see-ers" who lead the advance of human thought, and so it is not strange that some of the clearest missionary messages of the Old Testament should be found in the Psalms, and the poetic visions of Isaiah. Humanity's gift of imagination enables a person to fuse the present and the future, the actual and the ideal, into one glowing vision, transcending experience. Tennyson could visualize the "Federation of the world, the Parliament of man," when as yet there was none of them. Kipling could describe the transatlantic voyage of a huge air ship, "The Night Mail," in what seemed to most people a mere fanciful tale. So David and the poets, out of the struggling earthly kingdoms, under the tutelage of God's Spirit, were able from afar off to rejoice in Messiah's reign and in the universal worship of Jehovah.

The poet, the real seer

Says Horton: "The story-teller, the poet, and the thinker give expression to the spontaneous feelings and aspiration of a people. . . . There can be no question that to find the real trend of a people you must examine the imaginative side of its life. If, for example, we wished to sum up the nineteenth century in England, we should feel that no parliamentary history and no legislative enactments would take us so surely to the heart of the question as the writings of Wordsworth and Carlyle, of Browning and Ruskin." So we shall find that while priest and Levite were poring over the minutiae of the Law, David with his harp, as he watched his flock on the hillside, was listening to the voice of the God who spoke through both Law and Prophet to the heart of humankind.

Ruth and Job in the missionary purpose

While the lawgivers were becoming constantly narrower and more bitterly nationalistic in their outlook, the men of imagination were writing the exquisite story of Ruth, the Moabitess, a woman outside the covenant, who chose God to be her God and his people, her people, and became an ancestress of Israel's Messiah King. Another great thinker was going to the Land of Uz to find an example of a true servant of Jehovah in the person of Job.

The Psalms are humankind's hymnal

But it is in the Psalms that the richest missionary meaning is found. If ever people were inspired by God's Spirit to write not for a nation, but for all humanity, it is surely the writers of the Psalms. These old hymn books of the Jews, written for the worship of the temple, have so little of ritual or particularity about them that quite simply and inevitably they express the universal heart of humanity. "Whoever were the human authors of the Psalms, the real author was the Spirit of God. No human poet or series of poets could have produced a collection capable of accomplishing such results as this has accomplished."

> These inspired poets give the breadth and inner meaning of the national institutions, that universal and eternal element which clothed itself for a time in the forms and methods of the Tabernacle and the Temple, but broke away from the old system when its day was over, to be clothed upon with the tabernacle from heaven, with that universal and holy religion which was suitable to the whole world.
>
> It would have been inconceivable beforehand how hymns could have been written in Judaism, to be sung in Christendom how the songs of the Temple, which was to be destroyed, could be suitable to the Temple not made with hands; how a community which was thinking only of its exclusive privileges and of its superiority to the other nations of the world, could unconsciously forecast a holy King, to whom all the nations of the heathen should be given, and compose the grateful praises in which a ransomed humanity would join. But that inconceivable possibility is precisely the miracle which is realized in the Psalms, and the missionary significance of it must be plain as soon as it is pointed out.
>
> *Horton*

Particular messages of the psalms

Turning to a brief consideration of a few of the many missionary messages of the Psalms, we find *a recognition that Jehovah is the God of the whole world*, King of people as well as of the material universe. See Psalms 2; 18:49; 19; 22:27-28; 24, 33, 46, 47, 65, 66, 67, 96, 98, 100, 117, 145.

A revelation of God to the human heart. Such Psalms as the twenty-third, the twenty-seventh with its rapturous "the Lord is my light and my salvation; whom shall I fear?" the penitent joy of the thirty-fourth, the proud trust of the thirty-seventh, the panting of the soul for the living God in the forty-second, the heart-broken cry to a God who forgives in the fifty-first, the overflowing gratitude of the one hundred and third, the help from the God of the hills in the one hundred and twenty-first, the overwhelming sense of God's presence in the one hundred and thirty-ninth, and the hallelujah chorus of the one hundred and fiftieth, are predestined to universality. They take the wings of the wind and fly to the uttermost parts of the earth; wherever a human heart is found they create their own agencies of transmission. The pure water of life from out the hills of God must find its way to the ocean of our need.

The vision of a messianic kingdom. There is in the Psalms a constant expectation and anticipation of a King who shall reign in righteousness over an everlasting kingdom. Doubtless many of these Psalms found their occasion in celebration of coronation or victory in the history of the monarchy. But any or all of the triumphs of David or Solomon, Josiah, or Hezekiah are far too small to fill the splendid canvas upon which the psalmist paints his glorious vision. Let any unprejudiced person carefully read Psalms 2, 22, 50, 67, 72, 80, 98, 110, and the conviction will be overwhelming that it is as prophet, rather than chronicler, that the poet is writing. Says Horton:

> The King of whom they sing is more God than man, and the dominion which is promised to him is humanity rather than Israel. Of course the national coloring is there, and the flights of fancy are sometimes brought down rather suddenly to concrete realities, before the poet's eye; but, as we put together the catena of those Psalms touching the King and the Kingdom, we know that we are dealing with a great missionary thought, which admits of no limitation short of humanity as a whole.

Jesus nourished his soul on the Psalms

Moreover, these very Psalms were part of those Scriptures on which was nourished the soul of the Son of Man. That he did not fail to find in them this nobler note of prophecy is very evident on turning to the Gospels. Matthew saw in Jesus' use of parables on that day by the seaside an echo of Psalm 78:2. Our Lord himself applies to himself the words of Psalm 118:22, 23 concerning the stone rejected by the builders (Matt 21:42), and to Judas the words of Psalm 41:9, about the betrayal of a familiar friend. As the disciples watched the figure on the cross during the dark hours of the crucifixion, it was of the words of the twenty-second Psalm that they thought as they saw the soldiers gambling for the garments of the Son of Man; and of the sixty-ninth Psalm as the sponge dipped in vinegar was thrust between his dying lips.

In his own perfect familiarity with the Jewish Scriptures, our Lord on the cross gave expression to his anguish and his trust in the words of Psalm 22:1 (Matt 27:46) and Psalm 31:5 (Luke 23:46).

The Psalms prefigured his experience

There are, moreover, several details in these messianic psalms which were exactly reproduced in the life of our Lord, although they are not so quoted in the New Testament.

Such, for example, are the words of attestation at his baptism and transfiguration (Ps 2:7); his rejection by his brethren (Ps 69:8); his condemnation by false witnesses (Ps 35:11); the piercing of his hands and feet (Ps 22:16), and the mocking of the crowd at his crucifixion (Ps22:7, 8).

Peter's and Paul's use of the messianic Psalms

Peter and Paul turned to the messianic Psalms for illustrations as they preached the risen Savior: Psalm 16:8-10 (applied Acts 2:25-31; Acts 13:35-37); Psalm 110:1 (applied Acts 2:32-36); Psalm 69:9 (applied Rom 15:3); Psalm 68:18 (applied Acts 2:33); Psalm 2:7 (applied Acts 13:33); Psalm 8:4-6 (applied 1 Cor. 15:27); Psalm 45:6-7 (applied Heb 1:8, 9); Psalm 22:22 (applied Heb 2:12).

(4) The missionary message of the prophets

The most glorious missionary messages of the Old Testament, however, are to be found neither in Law, history, nor poetry, but in the writing of the prophets, when "holy men of old spake as they were moved by the Holy Spirit."

The prophets seem our contemporaries

It must not be forgotten that the structure of the Old Testament is not linear, but rather on four parallel lines covering somewhat the same periods of time with differing emphases. Thus, the prophets accompany the poets, and they the historians, over a great part of Israel's pilgrimage. But while Chronicles narrates the story from the ecclesiastical point of view, the prophets are reacting to the same Providences in the light of spiritual and universal applications of the moral law. This is what makes the prophets so contemporary. The quaint and archaic in the fashion of thought of those who wrote the Chronicles of the kings is wanting in the burning messages of the prophets. To us they speak with present authority; of our sins and problems they write; it is our faith that they reassure in the coming of the rule of God among humankind.

Missionary conceptions common to the prophets

There are certain great conceptions more or less common to the prophets: (a) They regard Israel as God's chosen instrument for worldwide ends; (b) They perceive in varying degrees the unity of human history; (c) They recognize God's disciplinary providences over his people; (d) They know that the chosen nation's privileges are not its property, but held in trust for humanity; (e) Their eyes are fixed not on the past, to see a vanished golden age, but on the future, with unquenchable hope. In this brief outline we can only hint at the missionary material of the prophets, in the hope that the suggestions given may lead out to more adequate study of the whole mind and heart enlarging subject.

Four prophets of the 8C B.C. There are four prophets belonging to the eight century before Christ,—Amos and Hosea of the northern kingdom of Israel, and Micah and Isaiah of the southern kingdom of Judah. In Amos and Hosea, the most ancient, explicit missionary lessons are naturally fewest; yet these two writers are outstanding figures in the development of human thought; their words contribute no slender stream to that river of the Water of Life that now runs wetly through all the earth.

The gospel in Amos Amos, a herdsman and gatherer of wild figs, appears suddenly before the luxurious and oppressive court of Jeroboam with a strong message from Jehovah. In words of rough-hewn and passionate sincerity he announces God's just judgment upon the surrounding nations, Damascus, Tyre, Edom, and Ammon, picturing the fate of Tyre, then in her glory. He lays bare Israel's oppression of the poor, the luxury and parasitism of her women, and prophesies famine and desolation. With wonderful tenderness he laments his country's fate and beseeches her in God's name to seek good and not evil, that she may live; to let justice run down as waters and righteousness as a mighty stream. With a social passion that we are wont to think belongs to our own day, he foretells the sure destruction and captivity to come, when God will sift Israel among all nations as corn is sifted in a sieve. His book closes with a majestic prophecy of restoration (Amos 9:11-15). The gospel's familiar lines are in the prophecy of Amos, faint, but clear: (1) Democracy in God's choice of an *instrument*; (2) Consideration for the poor at a time when pity was *unknown*; (3) God's righteous government reaching out to the whole world; (4) A spiritual as opposed to a ritual religious emphasis.

Hosea's gospel of the love of God Hosea is the earliest great teacher of the love of God. Through the teachings of his own sufferings because of an unfaithful wife, Hosea discerns the suffering love of God reaching out after his rebellious people. A new voice was heard in the world, one single thrilling note, when Hosea dared to figure the eternal as drawing his people with the cords of a man, with the bands of love, and to sound the note of God's heartbreak over his rebellious people. "How shall I give thee up, Ephraim? How shall I deliver thee, Israel? O Israel, thou hast destroyed thyself; but in me is thine help. I will ransom thee from the power of the grave. O death, I will be thy plague." A note new in the world, but to grow and increase until it culminated in the gospel of a God who so loved the world that he gave his Son to save it.

Micah foretells the coming kingdom

After Samaria fell in her unrepented evil doing, Micah and Isaiah took up the work of warning the southern kingdom of the fate that was sure to follow upon its godlessness and immorality. The conditions of industrial oppression and social vice which Micah reveals among the princes of Judah do not differ materially from those which Amos denounced in Israel or those which are to be found in our own day. Against them the prophet pronounced the sure doom which ever dogs the steps of the nations that forget God. In his fourth chapter is found the earliest clear forecast of that universal gospel at the heart of God's plan for his ancient people.

> But in the last days it shall come to pass, that the mountain of the house of the Lord shall be established in the top of the mountains, and it shall be exalted above the hills; and people shall flow unto it.
>
> And many nations shall come, and say, "Come and let us go up to the mountain of the Lord and to the house of the God of Jacob; and he will teach us of his ways, and we will walk in his paths; for the law shall go forth of Zion, and the word of the Lord from Jerusalem.
>
> And he shall judge among many people, and rebuke strong nations afar off; and they shall beat their swords into plowshares, and their spears into pruning hooks; nation shall not lift up a sword against nation, neither shall they learn war any more.
>
> But they shall sit every person under their own vine and under their fig tree; none shall make them afraid; for the mouth of the Lord hath spoken it.
>
> For all people will walk every one in the name of his god, and we will walk in the name of the Lord our God for ever and ever.
>
> *Micah 4:1-5*

Micah's interpretation of true religion

In Micah, too, occurs the remarkable prophecy in regard to Bethlehem (Mic 5:2) and the most glorious setting forth of spiritual as opposed to formal religion; an interpretation of religion absolutely fatal to any partial, racial, or dispensational claims, and embracing all humankind under its wide sky.

> Wherewith shall I come before the Lord and bow myself before the high God? Shall I come before him with burnt offerings, with calves of a year old?
>
> Will the Lord be pleased with thousands of rams, or with ten thousands of rivers of oil? Shall I give my firstborn for my transgression, the fruit of my body for the sin of my soul?
>
> He hath showed thee, O man, what is good; and what doth the Lord require of thee, but to do justly and to love mercy, and to walk humbly with thy God?
>
> *Micah 4:6-8*

The circumstances of Isaiah's ministry

Isaiah has been called the fifth evangelist, because in his prophecies the gospel note sounds clearest and most often. What were but scattered gleams and intimations in Hosea and Amos become settled convictions with Isaiah. In his writings for the first time we recognize a world vision. Isaiah lived and prophesied through four invasions of Judea, by the insolent and brutal power of Assyria. He lived when all the little nations of Western Asia alternately trembled and intrigued between the great world powers of that day; Assyria to the North, Egypt to the South. Judah was Assyria's Belgium, lying between her ambitions for world domination and her rival, Egypt.

Two convictions underlying Isaiah's gospel

Isaiah's missionary meaning rests upon two convictions; God's righteousness and God's providential government not alone of his chosen people, but of the world. In his superb confidence in the might of God's righteousness, he is able to reassure the hearts of his generation, paralyzed by the fear of a conscienceless tyranny. The first expression of the Christian philosophy of history was given in Isaiah's claim for Jehovah of an authority over all the nations, to use them as instruments to work out his providence.

One Lord over all nations

In the "dooms" pronounced upon all the nations surrounding his own, Isaiah breaks in upon the exclusiveness of his people with a new world note. "As you read his prophecies upon foreign nations," says George Adam Smith, "you perceive that before the eyes of this man humanity, broken and scattered in his day as it was, rose up, one great whole, every part of which was subject to the same laws of righteousness and deserved from the prophet of God the same love and pity."

Isaiah takes possession of the world in God's name

From his watch tower of prophecy Isaiah looked out upon a world that seems strangely small to our modern eyes; but a world that filled the largest horizon of those times, a world stretching from the ultimate West of the Isles of the Aegean to the ultimate East beyond the great river Euphrates. Of this world he took possession in the name of God; looking forward to the time when "the particular religious opportunities of the Jew should be the inheritance of humanity." In closing one of the noblest missionary sermons of the Old Testament, he writes: "In that day shall Israel be the third with Egypt and with Assyria, a blessing in the midst of the earth; for that Jehovah of hosts hath blessed them, saying, 'Blessed be Egypt my people and Assyria the work of my hands, and Israel mine inheritance.'" (Isa 19:24-25)

Isaiah's challenge for today

The same questions as those Isaiah faced are still at stake. Men are still in danger of believing in the right of might, rather than the might of right. Deep cleavages still divide nations, making it difficult to believe in one Father God with a purpose that embraces all humankind. Still are men fain to settle down in selfish ease when no foe menaces their own frontier, forgetful of those others without the gate for whom Christ died. For the Christian church of today, as for God's ancient Jewish people, Isaiah has a message. We, too, must in the name of God claim the world for our parish. A modern writer has phrased this missionary challenge in unforgetable terms.

If missions fail, Christ a failure

"I am asked, 'do you believe in foreign missions?' I answer, 'Do you believe in the gospel of Christ?' For be assured of this, if foreign missions, when considered in the large, are a failure, the gospel is a failure. If Jesus Christ has no message for the one in Shanghai that is worth giving my life, if need be, to get it to that person, he has no message for the one in London that I need bother about. He is either the Savior of the whole world or he is no one's Savior."

Other instances of Isaiah's vision of the world-meaning of his nations' faith may be found in chapters 2; 9:2-8; 33.

The vision of the Suffering Servant

The latter chapters of the book, the fortieth to the sixty-sixth inclusive, have been called "one glowing rhapsody of Zion redeemed." Internal evidence of this portion of the prophecy has led many reverent students of the Bible to assign the prophecies to a later date and to another author. Whether this or the traditional view is taken does not alter the glorious missionary message of these marvelous prophecies. The ideas underlying the earlier chapters are here expressed with a fullness and a glory of prophetic hope that put them on a plane nearer to the New Testament than any other portion of the Old Testament. Not only are the righteousness of God and his nearness to his people discerned, not only is Jehovah proclaimed as the God of the whole earth, but the vision of the Suffering Servant of Jehovah is so drawn that the heart of the world has recognized in it the portrait of the one who was, indeed, wounded for the transgressions of the whole world. See Isa 42:1-4; 52:7, 10, 15; 60:1-9; 61:1-3, 11; 65:1; 66: 10, 12, 13, 16, 18-23.

The call of the prophet Jeremiah The prophet Jeremiah delivered his message during the terrible days of the dissolution and exile of his nation. His was the hard task of doing a patriot's duty in such a way that to the people of his day he seemed false to his country. In Jeremiah's call we have a noble prototype of the call of all true missionaries. Summoned out of his conscious weakness, girded with the power of the God who commissioned him, he is sent to "nations and kingdoms, to root out and to pull down, to destroy and to throw down, to build and to plant" (Jer 1:10). Thus ever does the task of destroying the false precede and accompany the constructive work of laying the foundations of the unseen empire of Jesus Christ.

Jeremiah, a type of the Suffering Servant In his personality Jeremiah stands out as the greatest of the prophets, the one who typified in his suffering on behalf of his sinning people that other who came as God's missionary to his own, but whose own received him not, who was rejected and made of no reputation among his brethren, and who wept over Jerusalem, still rejecting the love of God, who sought her. Out of the agony of his witnessing Jeremiah comes to hope in the coming King in his kingdom. See Jer 23:1-8; 31:10-12, 31-34.

Ezekiel's gospel for the individual Ezekiel is the great prophet of the captivity, writing out of the land whither the exiled people had been taken. In Ezekiel we have the emergence of the gospel for the individual. The elder prophets, and even Isaiah and Jeremiah, fixed their thought for the most part on God's purpose for the nation and, through the nation, for the world. Ezekiel writes his message of hope and restoration to the nation, but he writes also for the individual. In one of the weightiest utterances in the history of religions, Ezekiel makes use of an ancient proverb,—"The fathers have eaten sour grapes, and the children's teeth are set on edge,'—to declare the eternal's care for every human soul.

> Behold, all souls are mine; as the soul of the father, so also the soul of the son is mine: the soul that sinneth, he shall die.

On this as his text he proceeds to build up his great discussion on heredity and environment, leading up to a conviction that lies at the very heart of the good news which Jesus came to give to all humankind. See Ezek 18:31-32; 11:19, 20; 36:25-27.

Not lost in the crowd, the gospel's glorious promise

This gospel of redemption for the individual is one of the most precious treasures of Christianity. The righteous individual is not lost sight of in a worthless family. The wicked has held out to him the promise of that new heart which is the gift of God. Such good news of salvation, like all good news, compels its own telling. It can no more be monopolized than sunshine or the stars.

In Ezekiel's parable of the hireling shepherd (chap. 34), is to be found a missionary message that rebukes our selfish ease as it did that of the professedly religious in the long ago. Can it be that America, called to be a shepherd nation, will close her eyes to Christ's flock, scattered shepherdless upon all the face of the earth, with none to search or seek after them? See Ezek 34:9-11.

These words were echoed long after by the Lord Jesus when he said, "Other sheep I have which are not of this fold; them also I must bring, and there shall be one flock and one shepherd."

The healing waters

The vision of the healing waters that flowed out of the sanctuary (Ezek 47:1-13), is a symbol of the progress of the gospel throughout all lands. Issuing as a slender stream from out the house of God, it deepens and widens until it becomes water to swim in, a river that can not be crossed over; and, into whatever desert the river flows, there come trees of fadeless leaf and fruit which shall be for food and medicine, and everything shall live whither the river cometh.

Speaking peace to the heathen

In Haggai and Zechariah we have the heathen messages regarding the rebuilding of the temple and the city from which truth shall go forth over the wide world. Zechariah has become forever precious to the Christian conscience in his foreshadowing of the betrayal and crucifixion of our Lord (Zech 11:12, 13; 12:10). He joins in the great chorus of the prophets to invite all nations to share with the chosen people in the grace of God (Zech 2:11; 8:7-8) and most gloriously, Zechariah 9:9-10:

> Rejoice greatly, O daughter of Zion; shout, O daughter of Jerusalem: behold, thy King cometh unto thee: he is just, and having salvation; lowly, and riding upon an ass, and upon a colt the foal of an ass.
>
> And I will cut off the chariot from Ephraim, and the horse from Jerusalem, and the battle bow shall be cut off: and he shall speak peace unto the heathen: and his dominion shall be from sea even to sea, and from the river even to the ends of the earth.

Habakkuk's message

Habakkuk's message seems peculiarly meant for our day. Baffled by the wrong and insolent tyranny which he beholds everywhere, the sensitive soul of the prophet turns to his God with a question: "How long will Jehovah permit wrong and violence to triumph, so that the Law is paralyzed and justice never gets done? Shall the oppressor forever draw his sword and ceaselessly massacre the nations?" And Jehovah answers: the prophet sets his answer down quite plainly, so that he that runs may read:

> It is God himself who is about to raise up the Chaldeans, that bitter and hasty nation, swifter than leopard and more fierce than evening wolves, and use them for his own purposes.

The everlasting yea

The poet's faith climbs trembling to the Holy One of Israel: "Hast thou ordained them for judgment? And O, Mighty God, hast thou established them for corrections? O why dost thou, who art of purer eyes than to behold evil, look upon those who deal treacherously upon his little watch tower of faith, looking for and keep silence when the wicked devour men more righteous than they, catching them like fish in their cruel net?" Again Jehovah answered his agonized prophet upon his little watch tower of faith, looking for evidences that:

. . . behind the dim unknown
Standeth God within the shadow
Keeping watch above his own.

God's answer is the quiet "Hush, my child," of the eternal.

Though the vision tarry, wait for it.
The just shall live by his faith.

Just the old, old riddle of the world, so torn and sinful, in which somehow the wrath of humanity is made to praise God, and his will gets itself done in spite of Assyrian or Chaldean, Attila, scourge of God, or the insolent rage of the Hun.

"Thy kingdom come"

The prophet, comforted, though not answered, raises the bold challenge of faith against all insolent evil of whatever age. Sure of the downfall and confusion that await every wicked work, the prophet sees

That the glory of God shall cover the earth as the waters cover the sea
See also Hab 2:14.

and in his renewed faith cries,

But the Lord *is* in his holy temple:
Let all the earth keep silence before him.

Out of what littleness are we come to what a wide expanse, from the days when Israel thought jealously of her God in his temple on Mount Moriah to this theophany of God who makes wicked nations his instruments of justice and correction, and before whom the earth keeps reverent silence!

The messages of the covenant

Of the "pointing prophets" in Sargent's great picture Malachi stands nearest, a messenger who tells the petulant people how the Lord will "suddenly come to his temple, even the messenger of the covenant, whom ye delight in: behold, he shall come, saith the Lord of hosts. But who may abide the day of his coming? And who shall stand when he appeareth? For he is like a refiner's fire, and like fullers' soap: and he shall sit as a refiner and purifier of silver: and he shall purify the sons of Levi, and purge them as gold and silver, that they may offer unto the Lord an offering in righteousness" (Mal 3:1-3).

> But unto you that fear my name shall the Sun of righteousness arise with healing in his wings: . . .
>
> Behold, I will send you Elijah the prophet before the coming of the great and dreadful day of the Lord.
>
> *Malachi 4:1, 5.*

"My name revered among the nations"

The most striking missionary teaching of Malachi is founding the first chapter, in which the prophet contrasts the grudging and polluted offerings of the priests with the worship offered to God outside the borders of Israel. The insertion in the authorized version of the words "shall be" in the eleventh verse, thus making the statement a prophecy, has obscured the meaning of the prophet. George Adam Smith's faithful translation makes it beautifully plain:

> A son honours a father, and a servant his lord. But if I am Father, where is My honour? and if I am Lord, where is reverence for Me? saith Jehovah of hosts to you, O priests, who despise My Name. Ye say, "How then have we despised Thy Name?" Ye are bringing polluted food to Mine Altar. Ye say, "How have we polluted Thee?" By saying, "The Table of Jehovah may be despised"; and when ye bring a blind beast to sacrifice, "No harm," or when ye bring a lame or sick one, "No harm." Pray, take it to thy Satrap; will he be pleased with thee, or accept thy person? saith Jehovah of Hosts. But now, propitiate God, that He may be gracious to us. When things like this come from your hands, can He accept your persons? saith Jehovah of Hosts. Who is there among you to close the doors of the Temple altogether, that ye kindle not Mine Altar in vain? I have no pleasure in you, saith Jehovah of Hosts, and I will not accept an offering from your hands. For from the rising of the sun and to its setting My Name is glorified among the nations; and in every sacred place incense is offered to My Name, and a pure offering; for great is My Name among the nations, saith Jehovah of Hosts. But ye are profaning it, in that ye

> think that the Table of the Lord is polluted, and its food contemptible. And ye say, What a weariness! And ye sniff at it, saith Jehovah of Hosts. When ye bring what has been plundered, and the lame and the diseased, yea, when ye so bring an offering, can I accept it with grace from your hands? saith Jehovah. Cursed be the cheat in whose flock is a male beast and he vows it, and slays for the Lord a miserable beast. For a great King am I, saith Jehovah of Hosts, and My Name is reverenced among the nations.

Was it reverenced by Jewish exiles? This passage may be understood in either of two ways: (1) that the "reverencing of God's name among the heathen from the rising of the sun to its setting" may be due to the spread of the Jewish Scriptures and religion throughout the ancient world. We know that the demand for a translation of these Scriptures was so great that one called the Septuagint was made into Greek in the third century B.C. We know, too, that this came into more general use than the original Hebrew, so that our Lord and his apostles, in quoting from the Old Testament, used the Septuagint. The wide diffusion of the Hebrew faith may be inferred also from the multitude of pilgrims who came annually to Jerusalem from every land to attend the Passover (Acts 2:1-11).

In every nation (2) On the other hand, the passage may be the acknowledgment on the part of the prophet that the one true God had those who served him in spirit and truth, all over the world, even as Paul said, "In every nation that feareth God and worketh righteousness is accepted of him." "From the first," says George Adam Smith, "they (the prophets of Israel) had known their God as a God of grace so infinite that it was impossible that it should be exhausted upon themselves. If his righteousness, as Amos showed, was over all the Syrian states, and his pity and power to convert, as Isaiah showed, covered even the cities of Phoenicia, the great evangelist of the exile could declare that he quenched not the smoking wicks of the dim heathen faiths."

The prophet Daniel When we turn to the book of Daniel we find ourselves on one of the battlegrounds of interpretation. The apocalyptic elements of Daniel's vision and those in the prophecy of Ezekiel form the background of John's glowing Apocalypse with which the New Testament closes. The diverse theories regarding the meaning of those apocalyptic elements are almost as numerous as the commentators. Such speculations are quite apart from the purpose of this brief survey, as are other disputes in regard to the date of composition. Whether the book of Daniel, as we now have it, is of single or composite authorship, we know that all of it was written before the translation of the Old Testament into Greek, during the third century, B.C. Its missionary message may be found by both radicals and conservatives.

The stone that became a great mountain

In the second chapter there is an account of Daniel's interpretation of a dream of Nebuchadnezzar, which none of the king's astrologers or sorcerers could interpret. The king dreamed of a great image with head of gold, breast and arms of silver, belly and thighs of brass, legs of iron, and feet part iron and part clay. Then he dreamed of a stone cut out without hands, which broke the great image in pieces like the chaff of the summer threshing floor, but the stone became a great mountain and filled the whole earth. Our attention is fixed not on what Daniel says about the four earthly kingdoms that shall arise in succession, but on his prophetic declaration that upon the destruction of the fourth kingdom:

> In the days of these kings shall the God of heaven set up a kingdom, which shall never be destroyed: and the kingdom shall not be left to other people, but it shall break in pieces and consume all these kingdoms, and it shall stand forever. Forasmuch as thou sawest that the stone was cut out of the mountain without hands, and that it break in pieces the iron, the brass, the clay, the silver, and the gold; the great God hath made known to the king what shall come to pass hereafter: and the dream is certain, and the interpretation thereof is sure.
>
> *Daniel 2:44-45*

The great expectation

Here we have reiterated the great hope that we have found expressed with varying degrees of clearness in all the prophets—the hope of a messianic kingdom. This indubitable fact is one of the mysteries in human history. Why should the Jew have cherished it, unless it were given by that Spirit of God who was speaking in the hearts of men? This expectation, phrased in such noble imagery, was fulfilled in the days of the breakup of Rome's kingdom of iron and clay, when the Lord Jesus came preaching in Galilee, "The kingdom is at hand."

Obscure elements Of the obscurer elements in Daniel's vision it is not necessary to speak. Since our Lord himself declared that he did not know "the day or the hour," we can hardly expect to learn it by calculations based on Daniel's prophecy. What is dark to us now may some day be made plain, but one thing is plain, the confident looking forward to the reign of the Son of Man in power. Through all the obscurities of apocalyptic vision certain promises shine out like stars; by them we may guide our course until the night is gone.

The prophet of Pentecost The prophet Joel has left us one of the noblest visions of the Old Testament in his prophecy of the pouring out of the Spirit on all humanity, so that old men shall dream dreams and young men shall see visions, and even upon the servants and the handmaidens shall the Spirit be poured out. In the great experience of the Day of Pentecost the disciples realized a fulfillment of this prophetic expectation. But that was only the beginning of fulfillment. In every land the Holy Spirit is today giving power to speak for God and witness for Christ. In the long dispensation of the Holy Spirit grace is poured out upon all people.

Jonah the missionary It remains to speak of a prophet whose book is in many respects the culminating message of the Old Testament. While men have gaped at the whale, they have quite overlooked the lesson which the story is meant to teach, whether we belong among the severe literalists, or to the company of those who understand the prophet to be making use of a parable or allegory to enforce the truth committed to him. Since questions of biblical criticism are outside the purpose of this brief study, let us dismiss from our minds any question regarding the setting of the tale, and go at once to the missionary heart of it.

A text for Jonah's prophecy Acts 11:18, might well be taken for the text of the sermon, "God has granted the gentiles also repentance unto life."

Jonah runs away from God Nineveh, the great, had already fallen suddenly, irretrievably from her imperial power,—a fall to which the sudden collapse of Vienna offers only a feeble analogy,—when Jehovah purposed to send a message of mercy to the citizens of this heathen city by the mouth of the prophet Jonah. Jonah arose to flee, not from the perils of the journey, but because, as he said, he knew the nature of the God who was sending him forth, "A God gracious and tender and long suffering, plenteous in love and repenting of evil," and feared that God might actually make him the agent of his grace upon the heathen. Jonah started to go to the ultimate West, the end of the Mediterranean, to get away from his hated mission. The hound of heaven, God's hurricane, pursued the runaway and flung him, repentant, into the sea and into the belly of a great sea monster whom God had prepared. Out of the depths Jonah cried unto his God and was delivered to be sent for a second time on the mission which he had refused.

God's purpose in Nineveh

Though outwardly obedient, Jonah was not in spirit reconciled to God's great purpose of mercy to the inhabitants of a city that had not known God's name. The repentance of the men of Nineveh which followed upon Jonah's summons, had as its purpose, according to George Adam Smith, to teach the chosen people that "out there, beyond the Covenant, in the great world lying in darkness, there live, not beings created for ignorance and hostility to God, elect for destruction, but men with consciences and hearts, able to turn at His Word and to hope in His Mercy—that to the farthest ends of the world, and even on the high places of unrighteousness, Word and Mercy work just as they do within the Covenant."

The irony of God

And the prophet, looking upon the effect of his message, was not glad but grieved, jealous that the God, the covenant God of Israel, was admitting others to his mercy. Over the peevish prophet God caused a great gourd to grow as a shade from the fierce sun, and then shriveled it with destruction. To the fainting prophet grieving over the loss of his gourd, God spoke in words of gentlest irony; "Thou carest for a gourd for which thou hast not travailed, a thing that came in a night, and shall I not care for Nineveh, that great city in which there are more than twelve times ten thousand children (persons that can not discern between their right hand and their left hand) and also much cattle?" Thus does God vindicate his boundless love and pity for all creatures that he has made, to the jealousy which would appropriate such love and pity even for the chosen people.

We have our Nineveh

If ever an age needed the missionary message of the book of Jonah, it is our own. The physical barriers between the nations are down. We may take ship to Tarshish and dwell in the uttermost parts of the earth, but still our jealous hearts are slow to believe in a God of the whole world. That God has purposes of mercy toward England and America, we know, but that Japan and China, too, are within the circle of his plan, we seem to question. It is a great thing to discover in the Old Testament, in the days of men's ignorance, a purpose that includes Jew and Gentile in its ample folds, a revelation of a message for all people.

III. Summary of ground covered

Reviewing the ground already covered, we have found in the very nature of the Bible a missionary charter; and in its teachings a plan of the ages, evident in the Old Testament, clearly revealed in the New. In a brief survey of the various divisions of the Old Testament Scriptures, we have found definite missionary lessons in every part, but most clearly wrought out in the Psalms and the prophets. These missionary teachings we have seen include: (1) A statement of the blessing for all the race held in trust by the chosen people; (2) A growing belief in the coming of a universal kingdom of God under the sway of a messianic ruler; (3) The universality of the providential government of God among the nations; (4) The emergence of a message for the individual believer as well as for the nation; (5) The distinct teaching that heathen nations are instruments of God; (6) The preaching of God's purposes of mercy to those outside the law; (7) The sudden coming of the messenger, and the setting up of the kingdom of God.

Outline
Chapter 2

AIM: To show that the missionary principles laid down in the Old Testament are fully revealed in the New in the fundamental teachings of Jesus; in his life; and in his commands to his disciples; and that these principles are exemplified in the life of the Apostolic Church.

Rooted in the Old Testament, the New blossoms with glorious intimations of universality in the very setting of Jesus' life. Its missionary message is found,

I. In the Two Fundamental Revelations of Jesus

1. *His disclosure of God the Father,* transcendent as well as immanent; righteous as well as loving; just as well as forgiving; fatherly to all men; a Father to his filial sons
2. *His teaching about the kingdom of heaven*
    a. Kingdom of heaven no new idea
    b. Cherished as noblest hope of Judaism
    c. Nature of Christ's teachings about the coming of the kingdom—not by revolution, but by silent transformation; not a national privilege, but a universal hope
    d. The kingdom at hand—Why then does it tarry? It need not tarry

- e. The delayed triumph of the kingdom implied in his parables
- f. How pass the long night of waiting? With loyal obedience, subordination of all else to the kingdom; with calm confidence in the ultimate triumph of the kingdom; with eager longing for its speedy consummation

II. In the Life and Direct Commands of Jesus

1. *Jesus was himself a missionary*
   - a. His first evangelizing tour—woman of Samaria; seed sowing and harvest
   - b. Choice of twelve disciples
   - c. Training and sending out of the twelve
   - d. Enlarging circles of ministry
   - e. Establishing a base line for the gospel
2. *Missionary commands of Jesus*
   - a. Missionary message not dependent on spoken command, but inherent in the gospel
   - b. Command four times repeated,—twice in Upper Room; on a hill top; just before his ascension

III. In the Apostolic Teachings and Life of Church

- a. Acts, the great textbook of missions—expansion of church; strategy of occupation; demand for heroism
- b. Paul's statement of missionary principles
- c. Emergence of missionary finance
- d. Lay ministry in the early church
- e. Prominence of women
- f. Fraternal and missionary spirit
- g. Missionary program of early church: An uplifted Christ; audacity of faith; participation in the task; reliance upon spiritual means; willingness to suffer or die; a buoyant hopefulness
- h. Missionary message of the apocalypse: written during terrible persecutions to encourage believers; presents Christ's triumphant kingdom; social passion of Christianity; doom of materialistic civilization; shining vision of New Jerusalem

Two

The Missionary Message of the New Testament

The Kingdom is an idea as broad as mankind, as inclusive as life itself, and as Christian as the Gospel.

Walter Rauschenbusch

From the twilight of the Old to the sunlight of the New

When we turn from the Old Testament to the New in our study of the missionary message of the Bible, it is like passing out of a dimly lighted room into glorious sunshine, or like walking beside a broad, deep river, after following a rill of sweet water. For the New Testament is missionary from beginning to end; in its plan, in its teachings, in its philosophy. In one flashing circlet John 3:16 includes the whole gospel: "For God so loved the world that he gave his only begotten son, that whoseoever believeth in him should not perish, but have everlasting life."

The New Covenant rooted in the Old

The missionary meaning of the New Testament grows out of the Old as a tree is rooted in the ground, as a rose expresses the sweet heart of the rosebud. One who reads the New Testament with no background of knowledge of the Old would punctuate many pages with interrogation points, and much of the finer symbolism of the book would be blank to him. Jesus based his gospel squarely on the foundation laid in the Old Testament: It was in the "fullness of time that God sent forth his Son, made of a woman, made under the Law to redeem them that were under the Law." It was in the consummation of an age-long purpose of mercy to all humanity that the good news was published abroad.

"Intimations of Universality"

This great purpose is clearly seen in the very setting of the life of Jesus. The promise of a coming salvation trembles through the words of the angel visitant to Mary and Elizabeth; and the joy of the Messiah so long promised by the ancient prophets throbs through the music of the Magnificat and the Benedicite.

"The heavens declare the glory of God"

When Jesus is born the very sky blossoms with angels singing tidings of a great joy which shall be to all nations; neighboring shepherds crowd about him, and splendid visitors follow his star from out the ancient East.

The gospel in the arms of the Law

In aged Simeon the Law seems to stand, holding the newborn gospel in its arms as he cries,

> Now, Master, though canst let they servant go, and go in peace, as thou didst promise for mine eyes have seen thy saving power which thou hast prepared before the face of all the peoples, to be a light of revelation for the Gentiles, and a glory to thy people Israel.
>
> *Luke 2:29-32 (Moffatt's translation)*

About him all nations cluster

The infant Jesus is carried into Egypt and returns to make his home, not in the royal city of David, but "in despised Nazareth." Among the crowds which follow him we find Romans as well as Jews, dispatriated tax collectors, Samaritans, Syro-Phoenicians, Greeks, and African Simon of Cyrene, a polyglot cross-section of humanity. Above him on the cross stood the inscription written in Hebrew, Greek, and Latin, in mute prophecy of the diffusion of his words among the nations.

Two centers of Jesus' thought

On this beautiful background of universality Jesus paints this gospel for humanity. There are two centers to his thought: (1) the Father God, whom he has come to reveal; and (2) the kingdom of God, which he has come to establish.

Christ's message of the Father

(1) We have already seen that the Bible teaching about God was in its very essence a trust for humankind. What is true in degree about the whole Bible is uniquely true about Jesus' thought of God. Above the revelation of the God and Father of our Lord

Jesus Christ hovers the very Shekinah of the New Testament. In that light all creedal and national and racial limitations disappear as the Son of Man unveils the eternal. The God and Father of our Lord Jesus Christ is none other than humanity's one true and living God.

Both Father and Lord

The modern thought of God has swung so far away from the Jewish thought of the transcendent holiness and absolute power and justice of God that it comes with a shock of surprise to us to find that our Lord, as Titus has said, did not emphasize God's omnipotence and infinite sublimity one whit less than did the Jewish view, but rather "deepened it and intensified it to the absolute uttermost." It is the Judge of all the earth, the God who "can not abide iniquity *and* the solemn assembly," the God who demands clean hands and pure hearts in his worshippers, and who is able to destroy both soul and body in hell (Matt 10:28) whom Jesus reveals as the Heavenly Father. "That is the paradox of Christ's revelation of God to us," says Hogg; "Fear and love,—love casting out fear; fear deepening and purifying love. Our Father, therefore, near us and in us; yet our Father in Heaven, and, therefore, at the same time absolutely exalted above us."

Over all and in all God, blessed forever

In the religions that emphasize God's immanence, as does Hinduism, men tend constantly to drift into pantheism, and to lose any clear conception of the blackness and power of sin, or the necessity of personal righteousness. In a religion that emphasizes God's transcendence, as does Islam, men tend to drift into formalism and fatalism. Only in the teachings of Jesus does humankind find a revelation of God infinite in holiness and absolute in power, who is also the Father, more eager than are earthly fathers to give good gifts to their little children, whose love, runs out to the prodigal while still in the far country, and whose Holy Spirit makes his dwelling place in the hearts of his humble worshippers.

God's fatherhood for all humankind

Jesus' teaching regarding the fatherhood of God has become so much the possession of our common thought that it is the general idea that the Christian message may be summed up in the phrase "fatherhood of God and brotherhood of man." It is, however, necessary to distinguish two senses in which the terms are used. (1) By the phrase "fatherhood of God and brotherhood of man" is generally meant that all people, being made in the likeness of God, are his offspring, sharing the divine nature, with the ineradicable stamp of his image on their souls, however blurred and faint that image may be.

> Though he is so bright and we are so dim,
> We are made in his likeness to image him.

Out of this common relation to our Father, God, springs the fact of human brotherhood, overleaping all barriers of race or nationality or social condition. This great truth is undoubtedly taught in the Bible, in the Old Testament by implication, in the New as the basis of our Lord's teaching and that of his apostles. The fatherly God who, through all the ages, has been going forth to meet his lost son while he was yet a long way off; the God in whom there is no respecter of persons, is that one from whom every fatherhood in heaven and earth is named.

God's true and filial sons

(2) But there is a deeper and more intimate, a more intensive and, therefore, less extensive sense in which the Lord Jesus uses the term, that has great force in considering the missionary message of the New Testament. Is there a sense in which Christ teaches that his disciples are sons of God and therefore brothers, which can not be affirmed of all people? A patient study of his words seems to establish this without doubt. It is a real spiritual union between God and individuals of which Jesus is speaking, and not of a possible or metaphysical relationship. It is the gentle, the forgiving, the merciful, the peacemakers, who are called children of God. It is those who love their enemies, do good to those who hate them, pray for their persecutors, that are the sons and daughters of the Father who is in heaven. It is those who do good and lend, never despairing, whom Jesus calls sons of the Most High, who is kind to the unthankful and evil. It is those who enter into their secret place of prayer, whose Father, seeing in secret, shall recompense; and it is whoever does the will of Jesus' Father in heaven whom he recognizes as brother, sister, mother. As John says:

> He came to his own creation, yet his own folk did not welcome him. But to all who did receive him, to them he has given the right of becoming children of God, even to those who trust in his name, who were born not of blood, nor of the will of the flesh, nor of the will of man, but of God.
>
> *John 1:11-12*

A new and living way to the Father

The missionary implications of this truth are momentous. Failure to perceive it is back of much indifference to the worldwide obligation of Christianity. Christ did not come simply to reaffirm a divine sonship in which all humanity shares. In that case we might rest quite tranquilly on the hope that sooner or later all would enter into the privileges of their sonship. He came to reveal a new and living way to the Father; to make possible a new and blessed fellowship with him, in order that through this new relationship he might establish the kingdom of God on earth.

The absoluteness of Christ's claims

Unless we understand the nature of this blessedness revealed in Christ, some of his own declarations may sound harsh to us.

> All things have been handed to me by my Father, and no one fully knows the Son except the Father, nor does any one fully know the Father except the Son and all to whom the Son chooses to reveal him.
>
> I am the way, the truth, and the life; no man cometh unto the Father, but by me. If ye had known me, ye should have known my Fatehr also; and from henceforth ye know him, and have seen him.

The riches of God in Christ

Their is no harshness here, but only a declaration of the exclusive claim on human reverence and obedience, inherent in the nature of the message. God's grace has found a way so to express itself through the person and words of Christ that the resources of divinity are placed at the disposal of humanity. It is in Christ we have our access, in Christ we realize our sonship, in Christ we put off the old life and put on that new life born from above; in Christ we who were dead in trespasses and sins are made alive by the power of God; in Christ the love of God is shed abroad in our hearts. This is what the New Testament calls the good news. This it is that we are commissioned to tell to the whole, wide world, that God was in Christ reconciling the world to himself.

Privileges of Christian sonship

From sheer familiarity with the privileges of Christian sonship, we fail to recognize their unique and precious character. As a matter of fact, the Christian consciousness of sonship is the gift of Christ. It does not exist apart from him. One of the glorious privileges of the missionary's life is to see the dawning of the new sense of sonship in the face of one who learns of its possibility for the first time. The consciousness of sin forgiven, of the warm, sweet, tender love of a Father, God, of springs of love rising in the heart to meet his great love, of a new brotherhood with our neighbor, these are the gift of Christ.

Christ's message of the kingdom

Growing out of Jesus' thought of God was his message of the kingdom. The term "Father" is found oftenest on his lips; but hardly less characteristic is the phrase "kingdom of God" or "kingdom of heaven." There are 122 passages in the Gospels that contain references to the kingdom; 55 occur in Matthew, 19 in Mark, 44 in Luke, and 4 in John. Many of these occur in parallel passages.

"Church" replaces "kingdom"

It is significant to note the change of emphasis that occurred later in the New Testament and in the church. The term "God, the Father," continues to characterize the other books of the New Testament, as it does the Gospels, although it is not used half so often in all the other books put together as in the Gospels. But another idea, "the church," replaces the "kingdom of heaven" in the attention of the writers of the New Testament. The kingdom is mentioned eight times in Acts, once in Romans, four times in First Corinthians, once each in Galatians and Ephesians, twice in Colossians, once in each letter to the Thessalonians, twice in Second Timothy and three times in Revelation.

The kingdom, no new idea

The missionary message of Jesus' teaching about the kingdom will become evident as we study a little more closely the meaning of the term. We note in the beginning that Jesus did not invent it. He simply used it. Neither did he define it, as would have been necessary, had he introduced an idea strange to the people. He took an old idea, widely held and deeply cherished, and enlarged and spiritualized it. Doubtless he had found the idea in the ancient Scriptures which he pondered so deeply and knew so intimately. It is fascinating to think of the boy Jesus reading words of Isaiah or Jeremiah. How the words would open to him "skyey meaning in which great promises shone faithfully like stars."

Popular understanding of the kingdom

What then was the popular understanding of the term "kingdom of God?" In the days of Christ there was a widespread expectation of a messianic kingdom which was shortly to be set up by the direct power of God. It was to be a new Jewish state in which God's Anointed, the Messiah, was to rule in righteousness. All Jews were to be members of the kingdom, and all other nations subject. Of its glories no pen could fitly write.

The noblest Hebrew hopes

Now this great thought of the kingdom had grown up through the ages of Israel's wanderings and sufferings. It meant different things to different minds; to Isaiah and the prophets it was a great spiritual hope; to the crowd it was often chiefly attractive for its material glories.

The kingdom hope shone brightest in the dark

It is one of the mysteries in the history of religion that the very catastrophes and tragedies in the life of Israel which seemed likeliest to have destroyed all faith in God did, as a matter of fact, arouse ever keener and more passionate anticipations of the coming kingdom. In it we may reverently discern the revelation of God himself to the soul of his chosen people. As ever fresh calamities overtook the nation, the prophet souls whispered, "Wait for the news of his coming. Soon and suddenly he whom we look for will come into his temple." The sense of immediacy had but deepened during the centuries until when John the Baptist appeared in the wilderness, renewing the proclamation of the prophets, all Jerusalem flocked out to hear him

Jesus proclaims the kingdom

After John had been thrown into prison, Jesus came into Galilee, proclaiming God's good news, and this was his proclamation: "The time has fully come, and the kingdom of God is close at hand; repent and believe the good news." That this was the subject of his preaching is shown in the summary which Matthew gives:

> Then Jesus traveled through all Galilee, teaching in their synagogues and proclaiming the good news of the kingdom, and curing every kind of disease and infirmity among the people.
>
> *Matthew 4:23-25 (see also 9:35-36)*

The nature of Jesus' teaching of the kingdom

Throughout the gospel narrative Jesus is engaged in teaching his disciples the true meaning of this kingdom of God which he has already set up among them. His teachings form the very heart of our Christian message. In this brief study it will be possible only to point out a few of them.

(a) Not a revolution;

Jesus refused to bring in the reign of God by a revolution. When He was tempted in the wilderness to choose the easy way of political revolution, rather than the hard way of the cross, he put it behind him; when the people tried to make him a king, he hid himself; to his disciples, eager for place and power in the new kingdom, he explained that the only greatness in the kingdom was service.

but a silent force

In our work for the kingdom of God it is most important that this phase of our Lord's thought about the kingdom be kept steadily in mind. The kingdom of God is, indeed, a revolutionary force in the world, but it is not to be set up by revolution. Silent and unseen as are all forces of the first order, the kingdom works within the soul of people and then, when the work is done, a new day is ushered in with all the miracle that attends the dawn.

Temptation to trust in lower methods

There is a constant temptation to forget this and to seek to win the world to Christ by the very methods he pushed one side; to trust to political reform, to social amelioration, to better environment (things all good in themselves, and to be desired), to bring the kingdom, and to despise or to overlook the very simple measures on which Jesus relied.

"And Germany had both"

Said a social worker in New York, "There are only two things needed to reconstruct the world." "What are they?" asked her friend. "Compulsory sanitation and universal education," was the answer. "Has it ever occurred to you," replied her friend, "that Germany had both in abundance?"

The might of meekness

The followers of Jesus can never expect to advance his kingdom by a resort to violence; they must always believe in the might of meekness, and seek to transform life from the center outward.

(b) Not a national religion

Jesus disappointed the high nationalistic and patriotic hopes of the people, and so blighted their budding loyalty. They were enraged when he pointed out to them in the synagogue at Capernaum that on the testimony of their own Scriptures God had reached out to show special mercy to the widow of Zarephath and to Naaman the Syrian. He commended the faith of the Roman centurion, saying, "I have not found so great faith, no, not in Israel." He raised a monument to the faith of the Syro-Phoenician woman. He angered and embittered all the orthodox of his day by his parables of the vine-dressers and the wedding feast. "The kingdom of God will be taken away from you and given to a nation that will exhibit the power of it" (Matt 21:28-46). He held up a hated Samaritan rather than the priest or Levite, as the good citizen. He spoke the deepest truths about his mission to a poor Samaritan woman by the well-side. Everything exclusive, haughty, selfish, or materialistic in the common idea of the kingdom he swept away. Imagine the wrath excited in patriotic breasts when Jesus said:

> There shall be weeping and gnashing of teeth, when ye shall see Abraham, and Isaac, and Jacob, and all the prophets, in the kingdom of God, and you yourselves thrust out.
>
> And they shall come from the east, and from the west, and from the north, and from the south, and shall sit down in the kingdom of God.
>
> And, behold, there are last which shall be first, and there are first which shall be last.

Christianity not the property of Anglo-Saxons

The Son of Man still goes about our streets, still rebukes our narrow ideas of his heavenly kingdom, still calls us to look up from our preoccupation with secondary truths, and look through his eyes of love at humankind. We are trustees of the gospel, not its owners.

Christ's message to John

When John the Baptist's faith failed him in the days of his imprisonment and he began to question the validity of the vision which was his on the great day when Jesus had come to him for baptism, he sent two of his disciples to, ask Jesus if he were in reality the coming one, or whether they were still to look for some one else. In this request of John it is evident that his faith is struggling with his preconceptions of what the kingdom of God ought to be like. It is to Jesus himself, that he takes his perplexity, a touching proof of his unshaken confidence in the character of the one whom he had fixed such glowing hopes. In answer Jesus quotes another prophecy of Isaiah, a part of the radiant vision of the coming kingdom contained in the thirty-fifth chapter.

> "Go and report to John," said Jesus, "what you have seen and heard; that the blind see, the lame walk lepers are cleansed, the deaf hear, the dead are raised, and the poor have the good news proclaimed to them. And blessed is every one who does not stumble because of my claims."

It need not tarry The missionary implications of this teaching of the kingdom are tremendous. In our Christian faith we have no simple system of ethics, no noble ritual of religious faith. We have a great overturning, transforming, revolutionary power to be released throughout the world. The kingdom now is. Its king is present, working by the Spirit of the living God on the hidden foundations of the unseen empire of Jesus Christ. With no littleness, no sectarian bitterness, no nationalistic limitations, all Christians everywhere are summoned to share in the works which our Lord taught us are the marks of his present kingdom. With all its imperfections the missionary cause is today accomplishing these messianic works among the nations on a scale large enough and heroic enough to enable the whole church of Christ to rejoice in what it sees and hears of the wonderful works of God.

The triumph of the kingdom to be delayed While our Lord teaches the possible immediacy of the Kingdom, he recognizes also its gradual coming and delayed triumph. The New Jerusalem coming down from God out of heaven is ever a "becoming," never a "being." In the Lord's Prayer itself we can clearly see that Jesus thinks of the kingdom as coming on this present earth, else why teach us to pray for its arrival, and also that it is not yet fully come, else why pray for it to come? Whenever we pray, "Thy kingdom come, thy will be done on earth as it is in heaven," we are asking for the continuance of a process, and for a hastening of the day of consummation.

Parables of the kingdom It is in his parables that Jesus states most fully the truth regarding the gradual growth and unfolding of the kingdom of God. The thirteenth chapter of Matthew records a group of parables regarding the "mysteries of the kingdom of God," spoken, many of them, as he sat in a boat near the shore of Galilee. In the parable of the mustard seed we have the growth of the kingdom from the least of all seeds to a great tree. In the parable of the leaven we have its hidden working in those three measures of meal (in which symbol Jesus included all humankind in one substance) "until the whole was leavened."

Jesus explains his parables Two of these parables, the sower and the tares of the field, Jesus himself late explained to his disciples. We find that by the seed he meant the Word of God, by the sower, the Son of Man, by the field, the world, and by the harvest, the consummation of the age.

"My lord delays his coming"

In the parable about the waiting servants (Luke 12:35-48) we have an intimation that the return of the Master may not be until the third watch of the night, and that in the long waiting the servants may grow careless and say in the heart, "My lord delayeth his coming." In the parable of the pounds (Luke 19:11-28) the nobleman takes his journey into a far country to receive for himself a kingdom, and to return. In the parable of the marriage feast (Matt 22:1-14), the whole long course of Jewish history is summed up under the figure of a day; it is not an unreasonable inference that the work of the servants whom the king sent out to find guests for the marriage supper may cover equally extended periods of time.

Intimations of long, watchful waiting

In the brief parable recounted in Mark 13:34-37, while the purpose is to inculcate watchfulness, there is again indicated the possibility that the coming may be delayed not only until "cock-crowing," but until "morning." Perhaps the clearest intimation in any of the parables is to be found in Matthew's great story of the ten talents (Matt 25:14-30). Here, too, the master, going on a journey, delivers his goods to his slaves and departs. Of his return Jesus states (verse 19), "Now, after a long time the lord of those servants cometh, and maketh a reckoning with them."

The seed growing secretly

Perhaps Jesus' thought of the growth and progress of the kingdom is best summed up in the parable of the seed growing secretly, which only Mark preserves: 4:26-30.

How pass the long night of waiting?

We are now in the period of germination, the long night of waiting. Christ has given to us each his task, and bidden us to occupy till he comes. With what attitude are we to face our life?

(1) *With loyal obedience.* "Thou sayest rightly, I am a king," said Jesus to the Roman governor, asking. He demands the loyalty of all those who would belong to his heavenly kingdom. No calling him "Lord! Lord!", no working of miracles will make up for the plain doing of his will. His kingdom belongs to the childlike, the gentle, the unselfish, the loving—only they can enter it. Disciples must take his yoke upon them and learn of him. To abjure self and take up the cross of sacrificial service is the price of following. There is no way to serve him except along the road of his commandments.

(2) *With subordination of all else to the kingdom.* The sternness of Christ's requirements that the kingdom is to be sought as the chief good of life is startling to those who have taken their ideas of him from mediaeval portraits. With regal authority Jesus claims the right of eminent domain for the kingdom of God. For it we are to leave home and family and country; in its service we are to endure hunger and cold and persecution and death itself, but "he who endures to the end shall be saved."

(3) *With calm confidence in the ultimate triumph of the kingdom.* Jesus never doubted this. The seed cast into the ground was to grow secretly; the hidden leaven was to work until the whole was leavened; lifted up, he was to draw the whole world unto himself; before him as king on his judgment seat were to be gathered all nations. He did not doubt in the wilderness; he did not despair on the cross; he bequeathed his joy and his peace to his disciples and bade them go forth with the good news, because all power had been given to him and he would be with them always.

(4) *With eager longing for the speedy consummation of Christ's triumph.* How faint is our hope, how languid our endeavor! We take it quite as a matter of course that the kingdom should tarry, and plan calmly on centuries of inch-worm progress. When a bold young spirit like John R. Mott arose a generation ago and with fiery logic actually proved to the church that the world could be evangelized in one generation, the church smiled indulgently at the impetuosity of youth, and refused even to take the idea seriously. Yet we have seen that Jesus did. With terrible earnestness he sent forth his disciples to hasten to the ends of the earth with good news that brooked no delay.

Hastening his coming

There is an expression in the second epistle of Peter that is very beautiful —"Looking for and hasting the coming of the Day of God,"—or in Moffatt's translation, "You who expect and hasten the advent of the Day of God." Expecting the day and hastening it! What a glory that gives to missionary work!

The world can be evangelized now

The war has given a worldwide illustration of how, under the pressure of unprecedented need, social processes and changes that ordinarily require centuries to effect have been accomplished literally in a day. In the great commonwealth of the kingdom of God there are greater possibilities waiting only the putting forth of a supreme act of faith on the part of God's people. The world *can* be evangelized in this generation.

From teachings to life

We turn now from considering the missionary message contained in the fundamental teachings of Jesus to (1) his missionary activities, and (2) his explicit commands contained in the Gospels.

"God had one Son, and he was a missionary"

(1) Jesus was himself a missionary—one sent with a message. In the delivery of his message he began by calling a group of disciples whom he took with him in his journeys as he proclaimed the good news of the kingdom. He evidently gained disciples, as we learn from the account of their baptism (John 3:22; 5:1-3). On his way from Jordan to Galilee he and his disciples stopped for a two days' mission in Samaria, during which the Samaritan woman and many of her fellow-citizens came to believe the gospel. In confessing their faith these men of Sychar use for the first time in history the great phrase that is in itself a missionary charter:

> We no longer believe in him simply because of your statements, for we have now heard for ourselves and we know that this man really is the *Savior of the world.*

Jesus' talk with the Samaritan woman

This brief missionary journey is notable also because it is the first proclamation of the good news of the kingdom beyond the limits of Jewry, and because of a saying of our Lord, recorded by John, when his disciples returned to find him sitting by the well curb, wrapped in the contemplation of his Father's glorious will for the world. In his conversation with the woman he had been led from depth to depth, to the announcement of his Messiahship, with its gift of the water of life; to the disclosure of the spirituality of the true worship of God: "neither in this mountain nor yet in Jerusalem, but in spirit and in truth"; and to the deepest truth of all, the seeking Father God. Now, withdrawn into the sacred recesses of his soul, he sits alone, meditating; may we not reverently imagine?—on the path along which the Father's will is to send his mighty gospel throughout the world.

"Look up and see the fields"

The disciples break in upon his solitude, anxious, hurried,

> "Master, eat something."
>
> "I have food to eat," said Jesus, "of which you do not know."

> "Can it be," said the literal-minded disciples, "that any one has brought him something to eat?"
>
> "My food," said Jesus, "is to do the will of him that sent me, and to accomplish his work."

Then, as if the nature of the work which the Father had sent him to accomplish swept over him, he turned and, with a gesture toward the sun-drenched plain across which the bright-turbaned throng was already hurrying out to him, he continued:

> Do you say, "It wants four months and then comes the harvest?" I tell you, look around, behold these plains—they are already white for harvest!

Sower and reaper together

Then follow the pregnant sentences in which our Lord explains that spiritual seed-sowing and harvesting proceed together, one man sowing, another reaping, and the sower sharing the reaper's joy. "I sent you to reap a harvest which is not the result of your own labors. Others have toiled and you reap the fruit of their toil."

Our waiting harvest fields

To his church of the present Christ still speaks these words. We, too, are apt to think of a remote harvest and to neglect the fields that lie all white to harvest under our very eyes. We, too, forget that in our work of spreading the gospel we are reaping harvests whose seed was sown by men long since dead, many of them obscure or unknown to us.

Jesus chooses twelve missionaries

With the opening of the Galilean ministry Jesus made a missionary circuit of all the towns of Galilee (Matt 4:23; 10:1-4). Later he chose twelve apostles, set them apart for missionary work, and gave himself to their training and preparation. It is due to an apparent accident of translation that these men are known to us as apostles rather than as missionaries. It means the same to say, "He chose twelve missionaries" as to say, "He chose twelve apostles." In one case the word is derived from the Greek, in the other from the Latin; both alike mean "one sent," "a messenger."

The twelve trained and sent out

On his second missionary tour Jesus takes the members of his Missionary Training School with him (Luke 8:1-3), and with them also go the members of the first Woman's Missionary Society. A third itinerary he makes, the twelve being with him (Mark 6:6; Matt 9:35), and then, their training being sufficiently advanced, he sends them out by themselves, two by two, on their first home mission enterprise.

The first "League of Pity"

Matthew tells us the touching reason for the organization of this first "League of Pity." When Jesus saw the crowds he was touched with compassion because they were distressed and were fainting on the ground like sheep without a shepherd. He said to his disciples:

> The harvest indeed is plenteous, but the laborers are few, therefore entreat the Lord of the harvest to send forth laborers into his harvest.

Enlarging circles of ministry

With this prayer in his own heart he sent them forth with marvelous instructions for their journey. Not yet did he send them to the Gentiles, their sympathies were too narrow, their prejudices too great. To the lost sheep of the House of Israel were they sent, while he himself continued his own tireless proclamation of the message, his own loving search for the lost sheep (Matt 11:1). Later, during the Perean ministry, the Lord sent out seventy disciples into every city and place where he himself intended to come, and this time he placed no prohibition on their going to the Samaritans and the Gentiles (Luke 10:1-4).

Establishing a base line for the gospel

In Jesus' own ministry he confined himself except in the case of a few individuals to his own nation. He was sent to establish a base from which his gospel could go out to the ends of the earth. While embracing in his love and purpose the world, he wisely spent himself on preparing a group whom he could so charge with his own spirit that through them the work for the whole might be done.

Mission strategy

This missionary strategy has its lesson for today. It is easier and more thrilling to scatter the gospel message broadcast over a province or a country; but the birds of the air very soon pick up such chance sowings. To a prepared people and then to a selected group within that people Jesus gave himself day and night, that from this garden of his planting he might sow the earth.

The missionary commands of Jesus (2) The direct missionary injunctions of Christ are in line with his teachings and his life. We quote more often and think more often of one which we call the Great Commission. When critics have called attention to the fact that the passage in which it occurs (Mark 16:15-20) is wanting in some of the ancient manuscripts, some have felt greatly disturbed. Whether the words belong to the apparently unfinished Gospel of Mark or have come down to us from some other source does not greatly matter, since like the exquisite little story of John 8:1-11, they bear all the marks of authenticity. It is hard to counterfeit the sayings of Jesus. They all bear his image and superscription.

Missionary message not dependent on "commissions" Even were the Great Commission, "Go ye into all the world and preach the gospel to every creature" absolutely blotted out, the missionary message of the New Testament would remain unshaken,—for there are other unquestioned commands of Jesus to the same effect. But even were all these lacking, the obligation to spread the gospel would lie with inescapable weight upon the Christian conscience. It does not depend upon enactment; it inheres in the nature of the gospel. We cannot imagine that those early Christians, scattered abroad during the first persecution, went everywhere spreading the good news of God's message because they remembered Mark 16:19 or Matthew 28:19. They told because their hearts were glowing in the consciousness of a great salvation and they could not but speak of what they had themselves seen and heard and felt.

Repetitions of Christ's great command The various forms of Christ's command to disciple all nations are found in Matthew 28:18-20; Mark 16:9-20; Luke 24:45-53; John 20:19-21; Acts 1:1-8. Each one is precious, each one adding a touch to the whole.

The command in the Acts We find from Luke's introduction to the Acts that it is his purpose to complete his former writing of what Jesus began to do and to teach by an account of his continued action through the Acts of the Holy Spirit. Luke tells us there that the topic of Jesus' lessons during the forty days intervening between his resurrection and ascension was the kingdom of God. The imagination loves to dwell on the wonderful way in which the victorious Christ opened up to the wondering minds of his apostles God's great plan of the ages by which through the life and death and rising again of his own Son, he was to make possible the salvation of the world.

Witnesses to the ends of the earth

Even after these marvelous days of ends of the earth teaching, the disciples still harked back wistfully to their early conception of a messianic kingdom set up by force.

> "Master, is this the time at which you are about to restore the kingdom for Israel?" they asked.
>
> "It is not for you," he told them, "to know times or epochs which the Father has reserved within his own authority; and yet you will receive power when the Holy Spirit has come upon you, and you will be my witnesses in Jerusalem and in all Judea and Samaria and to the remotest parts of the earth."

"The faith of the Lord Jesus"

Paul uses a great phrase, "The faith of the Lord Jesus." Never was it more greatly manifested than when, his earthly pilgrimage accomplished, Jesus gave his last charge to his disciples. He had no organized church, no buildings, no synods, no bishops; there was no treasury, no written gospel. On his naked faith in his Father and with confidence in those to whose memory he had entrusted his own teachings, Jesus sends them forth, his commissioned witnesses, to the ends of the earth.

The four zones of missions

The four zones are significant. There is Jerusalem—the place where we live; Judea—our native land; Samaria—our neighbor state, and those "uttermost parts of the world." Some one has named them parish missions, state missions, home missions, and foreign missions. All are there, present in the master's thought, provided for in his plan.

On a hill in Galilee, to the eleven

Matthew records for us the words Jesus spoke on the hill to the eleven whom he had summoned to meet him there. Though the record is very plain that the appearing and the command were to the eleven, most of us in our mental picture visualize the five hundred who, as Paul tell us, saw him at one time. If we picture on that hill in Galilee only the little company of men who had loved and known him best, and see the mysterious figure of the risen Jesus appear before them as they prostrate themselves in worship, it adds a wondrous touch of homely honesty when Matthew adds "but some doubted." No romancer could have thought of that touch. No one not an eyewitness could have added it. It is Matthew who remembers the shuddering joy with which they saw him, and then the questioning eyes which he and Thomas turned on the others when the radiant figure was no longer visible, saying, "Did we indeed see him? Did we not dream it?"

The Great Commission

No, the eleven remembered to their dying day the majestic words he spoke as he came near them:

> All power has been given me in heaven and on earth. Go, therefore, and make disciples of all the nations; baptize them into the name of the Father, and of the Son, and of the Holy Spirit; and teach them to obey every command which I have given you. And remember, I am with you always, day by day, until the close of the age.
>
> *Matthew 28:18-20 (Weymouth)*

The command is backed by power

This is the fullest report of any of the commands of Jesus given during the solemn ministry of the forty days. Note that the command is based upon power, "all power in heaven and on earth." "Go, therefore, because I have authority and power to send you." We need to recover more of the soldierly quality of obedience in our missionary service. These are our marching orders, given by the supreme commander to his generals with the full sanction of his authority behind them.

"What are your marching orders?"

"What are your marching orders?" questioned the old Iron Duke when someone asked him whether he believed in foreign missions. We are not asked whether we wish to go, whether it will do good to go, whether it is practicable to go. The king has summoned us. It is enough.

Promise is added to command

To the command with its backing of authority Jesus adds his gracious promise, "Lo, I am with you all the days." We often divorce the promise from the command, but there is a question about our warrant for it. It is to those who, trusting in his supreme authority, go forth in obedience to his command, that our Lord says, "Lo! I am with you always."

David Livingstone's journal

While battling against obstacles as tangled and impenetrable as Africa's own jungle thicket, David Livingstone wrote in his journal:

> Felt much turmoil in view of having all my plans for the welfare of this great region knocked on the head by savages tomorrow. But Jesus came and said, "All power is given to me in heaven and in earth. Go ye therefore and teach all nations, and lo, I am with you alway, even unto the end of the world!" It is the word of a Gentleman of the most sacred and strictest honour, and there is an end on't. I will not cross furtively by night as I intended. It would appear as flight, and why should such a man as I flee? Nay, verily, I shall take observations for longitude and latitude tonight, though they may be the last. I feel quite calm now, thank God.

Not orders alone, but a program

Our Lord's last words to the eleven give not only marching orders, but a program. In the brief compass of thirty-five words we learn to whom the disciples are to go—all nations; what they are to do—make disciples; what ordinance they are to perpetuate—baptizing them; what method they are to use— "teaching them to observe all things whatsoever I have commanded you." We have here the universality of the missionary message; its purpose of discipling the nations; its churchly organization and its educational and disciplinary content.

A preaching, teaching church

Those who would reduce missions to purely evangelical proclamation of the good news (Mark 16:15), find here an equally binding command to teach. Those who would make missions only social settlements and agencies for the diffusion of the blessings and benefits of modern civilization find here firmly embedded the perpetuation of one of the two ordinances left by our Lord to his church, and by a fair implication the implanting of the church itself. Rightly has this passage been called "The Missionary's Great Charter."

Luke's Gospel records the first worldwide commission

Luke's other account, given in the Gospel (Luke 24:45-49) refers to a different occasion from that recounted in the first chapter of Acts, as is evident from the ninth verse, in which we are told that, when Jesus had spoken these words and while they were looking at him, he was carried up and a cloud hid him from their sight. In the twenty-fourth chapter of Luke's Gospel, on the other hand, the evangelist is recording the first appearance of Jesus to the disciples, on that Sunday evening when the doors of the house were locked for fear of the Jews. The two from Emmaus had just come, breathless with their great news, and found that the story of the master's appearance to Simon had already preceded them. And, while all were talking and doubting and wondering, Jesus himself stood among them and showed them the nail prints in his hands and feet.

> Then he opened their minds to understand the Scriptures, and he said, "Thus it is written that the Christ would suffer and on the third day rise again from the dead; and that proclamation would be made in his name of repentance and forgiveness of sins to all the nations, beginning at Jerusalem. You are witnesses as to these things."

Repentance and forgiveness to be proclaimed to all nations

Here again the missionary accolade is laid on the shoulders of true Christian knights. The gospel is rooted in God's plan of grace for the whole earth. In the name of the risen Christ repentance and forgiveness are to be preached throughout the earth and the disciples are to be witnesses of the truth.

The innermost heart of the Great Commission

In John's Gospel there is preserved another word of Jesus, spoken on this very night, which contains the innermost heart of the missionary commission. "Jesus then repeated, Peace be with you. As my Father sent me forth, I am sending you forth" (John 20:21; Moffatt). The Great Commission is here given in its highest form. Not simply are the disciples to go forth with good news to all nations; they are given the same commission which Jesus himself received from the Father. Whatever he came to do they are to do; whatever his message was is their message; the width and height and length and breadth of his mission form the only boundaries to their mission. "As my Father sent me forth"—to the lame, the blind, the deaf, the poor, the prisoner, the stranger, the leper without the gate,—to them I send you forth. As my Father sent me forth "a light to lighten the Gentiles and the glory of my peoples Israel," so I am sending you forth. "As my Father sent me forth, not to be served but to serve," so I send you forth. "As my Father sent me forth, not that the world might be condemned, but that the world might be saved through me," so I send you forth. "As my Father sent me forth to endure the cross," so I am sending you forth, not to cling to my cross, but to carry it. "As my Father sent me forth to overcome the world," so I send you forth. Never were words more glorious spoken to human hearts than these. O, the breadth and the length and the depth and the height of Christ's meaning in his last and great commission!

Summary of missionary message of the Gospels

In summing up the missionary message of the Gospels we have found that it penetrates their entire structure; is a necessary outcome of the two fundamental teachings of Jesus regarding the Father and the kingdom; is contained in his parables and illustrated in his daily deeds; is explicitly stated by direct command given under circumstances of the utmost Solemnity, and that these final instructions were repeated at least four times: Luke 24:33-47; John 20:21; Matt 28:16-20; Mark 16:15-20; Acts 1:1-9.

Missionary message of New Testament outside the Gospels

When we turn from the Gospels to the rest of the New Testament we find that it consists of little else than the account of missionary journeys, letters from missionaries to their converts, and a prophecy of the complete triumph of the gospel.

The Acts: the great mission-study textbook

The Acts, written by Luke as an epilogue to his Gospel to show what Jesus "continued to do and to teach through the Holy Spirit," is the greatest textbook on missions in existence. Here we see the widening circles by which Christianity spread out from Jerusalem to Rome, the enlarging conceptions wrought in the minds of Christian believers regarding the scope of the gospel, the strategy of occupation devise by master missionaries, and the eternal conflict with evil which the gospel meets in establishing its worldwide sway. Here we find the substance of the missionary message that has power to win the world, Jesus Christ, Crucified and Risen form the Dead.

The expansive power of a new affection

Here we find that Christianity, when barely established in Jerusalem and Antioch, did not wait to complete the task of local evangelization, but pressed out into new fields by the irresistible power of its expanding life. Where is there a nobler corrective of the point of view of those who say, "There is plenty to be done at home," than in the example of that heroic pioneer church in Antioch which sent forth its two strongest leaders, Paul and Barnabas, on the summons of the Holy Spirit?

"There is that scattereth and yet increaseth" If counsels of self-interest and prudence had prevailed, Christianity would still be a struggling Jewish sect in the lands at the eastern end of the Mediterranean. But the missionary passion had free course and was glorified. Antioch, in giving her best to carry the gospel to distant lands, found her own spiritual strength renewed. It is due to no chance that the disciples were first called Christians at Antioch.

Missionary strategy of Acts In the book of Acts are lessons of missionary strategy of permanent value. These hurrying missionaries of the cross do not seek solitudes, but the crowded centers of life. In the chief cities of Greek and Roman culture and commerce they plant the first churches, and from these as centres the gospel seed is carried to the boundaries of the empire within a hundred years.

A summons to Christian heroism In Acts the summons is to the heroism of the crusader. The gospel is seen as no beautiful, ethical statement to be admired and written about. It is a desperate cause to be fought for and died for. Christ's message is presented not as something which wins easy acceptance, but as a challenge standing squarely athwart human selfishness and greed and sin, and so meeting deep hostility and opposition. The instinctive recognition, on the part of evil forces, of the gospel as a deadly foe is disclosed again and again in this mission textbook.

Only a compromising church finds smooth sailing When opposition fails to materialize in the life of the present day it is because the church is not aggressive in asserting Christ's lordship over life, as was this early church. A compromising church finds smooth sailing. A missionary church can always count on her full share of head winds and tempest.

Paul's statement of the universal gospel In Paul's letters we find a treasury of tremendous statements of the universal gospel. To instance but a few of them: Rom 1:16; 2:10, 11; 3:21-24; 3:29; 5:15-19; 10:11-13; 1 Cor 1:21-24, 2 Cor 5:18-19; Eph 2:11-18; 1 Tim 2:3-7.

Emergence of missionary finance There is evident also the emergence of the problems of missionary finance as the expanding work requires increased funds. Immediately following Paul's great declaration of the universality of God's grace, "Every one without exception who calls on the name of the Lord shall be saved," he finds it necessary to append a practical inquiry: Romans 10:14-45.

Giving money part of preaching the gospel

These words and those others of Paul in regard to the missionary contributions which he was gathering among his Gentile converts to take to the poor saints in Jerusalem have been read in innumerable missionary meetings, and have stirred many sluggish consciences in our days to realize that giving money is a part of preaching the gospel. See Romans 15:25; 1 Cor 16:1-21; 2 Cor 8:1-15; Acts 11:29.

Lay ministry in the early church

A beautiful sidelight on the fellowship of ministry which prevailed in the early church is found in the personal greetings with which Paul closes his letters. Here is reflected no hierarchy propagating the faith through solemnly official channels, but groups of men and women bound by one fraternal purpose. Phoebe is seen hurrying as a messenger from Cenchrea to Rome with the great epistle to the Romans safely hidden under her robe. She would seem to have been a woman of wealth and prominence. Paul tells us that "she has been a kind friend to many including myself." Then there are Priscilla and Aquila who have a church in their house, travel about on the business of the kingdom, and endanger their lives to help Paul. It is interesting that only once does Paul mention Aquila's name first; in all other allusions it would seem as if the wife were the real leader. In fact, the prominence of women workers in these early lists is little less than amazing, when the social customs of the times are considered.

Women workers prominent

There is "Mary who labored strenuously among you"; "Junia, my fellow citizen, who once shared my imprisonment"; "Tryphaena and Tryphosa, those Christian workers"; "dear Persis who has labored strenuously in the Lord's work"; and "Rufus' mother who has also been a mother to me."

Fraternal and missionary spirit of the early church

In nothing is the fraternal and missionary spirit of these early Christians more clearly shown than in these passing allusions in the epistles. We see them packing missionary boxes, sending a messenger seven hundred miles to take food and clothing to the missionary in prison at Rome, risking life itself in ministry to "the brethren." We love the abundant hospitality of Lydia and of "that household of Stephanus, the first converts in Achaia," who "laid themselves out to serve the saints." We see the strength of their brotherhood in that traveling band of believers, Sopater of Beroea (the son of Pyrrhus), Aristarchus and Secundus from Thessalonica, Gaius of Derbe, Timotheus, and Tychicus and Trophimus of Asia, who accompanied Paul in his return through Macedonia and then went on to wait five days for him at Troas. We see it again in the elders of the church of Ephesus, who came down to Miletus to see Paul and broke into loud lamentations as they kissed him farewell, sorrowing because they should see his face no more. Paul "tore himself away from them" only to meet another group of believers when the ship touched at Tyre, who escorted him outside the town, "women and children and all," and kneeled on the beach while Paul prayed with them and said goodbye. In Caesarea he was entertained by Philip the evangelist, who had four unmarried daughters who prophesied. When, "after a somewhat lengthy stay," Paul loaded his baggage-cattle and continued his journey to Jerusalem, disciples from Caesarea accompanied him on his journey and took him to lodge in the house of one of the early disciples, Mason, a native of Cyprus. See Acts 21 (Weymouth).

We are told that the brethren in Jerusalem gave Paul a hearty welcome. When he landed in Italy on his way to Rome the disciples in Puteoli invited Paul to stay with them for a week, and those living in Rome walked out to meet him as far as the Appian Forum and the Three Taverns.

Similar scenes enacted today

All these and other homely incidents picture to us the missionary churches of the first century. Similar pictures are to be seen on many a frontier where little bands of Christians area cheering one another's faith, as they hold the "thin, red line" of occupation for their master, Christ.

Value of missionary study of the Acts

The study of this missionary church, of the apostolic age is sorely needed; in the present age. The greatest danger of the missionary enterprise is that it may be officialized, externalized, becoming the cult of a group rather than the expression of the church's life. No missionary study can so powerfully counteract this danger as the study of New Testament Christianity both as interpreted by Christ himself, and in the life of the apostolic church.

(1) *An uplifted Christ.* Note the features of their missionary program. It was Christ who was the substance of their preaching, Christ who was their hope of glory, Christ whose was the power in which they dared face the

might of the Roman Empire. No missionary should be sent forth who goes to take a question, none who has not in his soul a personal experience of Christ's grace and redemption, "the inexpugnable reality of the life of God in the soul of humanity."

(2) *An audacity of faith.* These people actually expected to convert the world. They were eager to penetrate unknown regions. Their horizon was ever,expanding, their courage never daunted.

(3) *A participation in the task.* The early church did not alone support missionaries; it was missionary. It did not take pride in the heroic faith of the missionaries but feel that its own part was fulfilled if it paid the bills and listened with languid interest to the stories the missionaries told of *their* successes. These little churches were themselves missionary beehives. Everybody felt called to tell the good news.

(4) *A reliance upon spiritual means.* Prayer pervaded the life of this early church like fragrance. They really expected prayer to be answered, and they dared to pray for hard and difficult things. They walked in the comfort of the Holy Spirit, who honored their faith by working mightily through and with them. Foreign missions contemplate tasks impossible of realization if we are depending upon human resources alone.

(5) A *willingness to suffer and, if need be, to die.* One cannot read the catalogue of Paul's privations and sufferings (2 Cor 6:4-10; 11:23-30) without a fresh realization that Christ's kingdom can only be established at the cost of lives laid down. The enterprise on which we are embarked cost Christ his cross. We cannot win the world unless we are willing to pour out life and treasure.

(6) A *buoyant hopefulness.* Nothing can quench the joy of this early church; tribulation, or distress, or nakedness, or peril, or sword! Nay, in all those, these missionary bands are more than conquerors, for they know that nothing can separate them from the love of God in Christ Jesus their Lord. We, too, need this supreme confidence of hope in a conquering, because a risen and present Savior.

Missionary message of the Apolcalypse

The closing book of the New Testament, the Revelation of St. John, is a fitting climax to its missionary message. In one apocalyptic sunset it floods the Book with hope. The church had fallen on evil days. Persecution threatened on every side. Multitudes had been thrown into prison for the name; other multitudes had suffered exile. The brutal materialism of the Caesars blasted every green shoot of faith and goodness by its idolatrous worship of the emperor. The beloved disciple himself was banished to a lonely island. From this as from a throne he thundered a message to the fainting Christians; a message which they, familiar with the apocalyptic writings of the ancient Scriptures, could easily interpret, but one that would be meaningless to the spies of Rome. Think what this message must have meant to persecuted bands of Christians who met at dead of night in the dark recesses of the catacombs to hear it read. They might be trembling under the displeasure of the emperor whose nod meant life or death. John lifted their eyes to une who is Alpha and Omega, fe who is, and was, and evermore will be, the ruler of all. To each of the persecuted churches the glorified Lord writes a message with its promise to those who shall overcome, backed by almighty power. Far above the world of sin and struggle John bade them see the great white throne and him who sat thereon. Above the cries of human anguish he bade them listen to the chorus of praise rising to the Lamb that was slain from ten thousand times ten thousand and thousands of thousands singing about the throne. He made them realize that the day of the oppressor was short, that "the kings of the earth, the great men, the military chiefs, the wealthy and the powerful" who now were persecuting Christ's followers should hide themselves in caves of the mountains while they called upon the mountains to fall upon them, and hide them from the wrath of the Lamb. See in this connection Revelation 7:13-17.

Christ's triumphant kingdom

Through all the splendid symbolism of the poem runs this golden thread *Christ is living. He will never forget his own. He will cause the right to triumph.* Many of the veiled allusions which were plain to those who first read the words illumined by the flaming torches of their present circumstances are obscure to us; but the main lesson is plain, and carries its missionary message without spilling. In spite of enthroned evil, in spite of apparent failure and defection, the kingdom of Christ will triumph. It is a universal kingdom. Men come into it out of every kingdom and tribe and tongue and nation. Great voices in heaven are heard to prophesy,

> The sovereignty of the world now belongs to our Lord and to his Christ, and he shall reign forever and ever.

Social implications of the Apocalypse

The social implications of the book make the Revelation a great revolutionary document, one that would assuredly have met destruction at the hands of Rome had its full import been understood. God is the ruler of nations. His will is their supreme law. Great Babylon, the mother of harlots and of the abominations of the earth, shall be destroyed.

The doom of materialistic civilization

The terrific doom song of the eighteenth chapter, "Great Babylon is Fallen," could not have been obscure to those who knew Hebrew apocalypses and prophecies; but they could hardly have felt as we do the social passion that sweeps it all. This judgment of Babylon, "through whom the merchants of the earth grew rich because of her excessive luxury," this Babylon "who glorified herself and reveled in luxury with her cargoes of gold and silver, of fine linen, purple and silk and of scarlet stuff"; this Babylon who "trafficked in wine and oil and fine flour and wheat and beasts and sheep and horses and chariots and slaves *and the souls of men*"; do we not know her well? In one short hour, says the prophet, this great wealth shall be laid waste, when God takes vengeance upon her because of those slain souls crying to him from under his altar, "How long, O Lord, how long?"

The shining vision of the New Jerusalem

Beyond the vision of judgment meted out to all cruelty and oppression and brutal materialism John sees the fair shining of the new heaven and the new earth, and the Holy City, the new Jerusalem, coming down out of heaven from God, and hears the voice which says,

> God's dwelling place is among men
> And he will dwell among them,
> And they shall be his peoples.
> Yes, God himself will be among them.

This is the consummation for which we work,—a holy city, a new Jerusalem,—not the old Jerusalem that slew her prophets, the old Rome that debauched the nations, the old New York or London that traded in the souls of humanity, but a new city, coming down *out of heaven*, a new city in a new earth where God will make his dwelling among humankind.

Cooperatng with God for a new earth

The Old Testament begins with humanity in a garden; the New closes with humanity in a glorious city in which there needs be no church or temple, for God's own presence fills it, and the Lamb is the light of it. The Bible is always forward-looking. Its golden age is never in the past. A great hope blows across its pages. A divine adventure summons the souls of men to work together with God for the creation of a new earth in which righteousness, no longer pilgrim and stranger, is at home; and in which the Lamb for sinners slain is loved and worshipped by every heart.

> Will it never come, that age of light and purity of heart? Never? Let me not entertain the doubt. Surely there will some day be reached that Eternal Gospel promised in the New Testament.
>
> *Lessing*

> Come forth, out of thy royal chambers, O Prince of all the kings of the earth! Put on the visible robes of thine imperial majesty, take up that unlimited scepter which thy Almighty Father hath bequeathed thee; for now the voice of the bride calls thee, and all creatures sigh to be renewed.
>
> *Milton*

Part II

Outline
Chapter 3

AIM: To set forth the work of translators through whose labors the Bible has become the possession of the race; to trace the history of the early translations and versions, and to follow the missionary translators of the nineteenth century as they have grappled with the tremendous task of putting the Bible into hundreds of tongues, many of them never before reduced to writing.

I. Earliest Translations
   1. The Greek Septuagint B.C., and the ancient versions A.D.

II. Place of the Bible among Early Christians
   1. Highly honored
   2. Open to the laity
   3. Used in education of children

III. The Bible in Early Missionary Enterprises
   1. The Greek church makes the Coptic, Syriac, Ethiopic, and Gothic versions
   2. Missionary expansion in India and China
   3. The Gothic Bible of Ulfilas
   4. Decline of Bible reading in Middle Ages
   5. The English Bible

IV. Bible Translation in the Modern Missionary Movement
1. Bible wonderfully adapted to translation
2. Great numbers of translations (compared to other books, *The Pilgrim's Progress*)
3. Bible translations essential to missionary progress
4. Difficulties of Bible translation
5. Benefits conferred by Bible translation

V. Some Notable Translators
1. William Carey
2. Adoniram Judson of Burma
3. Robert Morrison, Schereschewsky, Wells Williams, and Gützlaff of China
4. Brown and Hepburn of Japan
5. Hiram Bingham, Henry Nott, John Williams, John G. Paton, and W. G. Lawes of the Pacific Islands

VI. Romances of Bible Translations
1. In Madagascar
2. In darkest Africa (Pilkington of Uganda)
3. The White Man's book of heaven
4. The Dakota, Navaho, and Cherokee Bibles
5. In Moslem lands

VII. Bible Triumphs of the Nineteenth Century
1. Translation of Scriptures a mighty achievement
2. Strategy of Bible translation

Three

All People in Their Own Tongue

The most important single agency in the work of evangelization is the Bible.

John R. Mott

Bible translation We have seen in the first two studies that the Bible in its nature and teachings is fundamentally missionary, a book built for humanity and carrying a message for all people. In the present chapter we shall study the process of translation by which the Bible itself became the active agent in the dissemination of Christian truth.

The Septuagint version The process of translation, as we have seen, began in the third century before Christ, when the Old Testament was translated into Greek, then the common language of trade, commerce, and intercourse between nations. With the wide dispersion of the Jews among the countries surrounding the Mediterranean, multitudes of them came to use Greek as their mother tongue. The influence and popularity of this version may be judged from the fact that the quotations from the Old Testament which appear in the New are for the most part taken from the Septuagint and not from the Hebrew original.

Earliest versions of the Christian era With the rapid spread of Christianity during the first three centuries there arose a demand for the translation of the Scriptures of the Old and New Testaments into the mother tongue of races that received the gospel. The earliest of these "ancient versions," as they are called, are the Syrian, Armenian, Coptic, Latin, and Ethiopic.

The Scriptures among early Christians

These early versions are an evidence of the exalted place which these early Christians gave to the Bible. Their Christianity was a living religion, an actively propagating faith. It could not do without its Bible. Jews were to be convinced that Jesus was the Messiah; and this could be done only through their ancient Scriptures. Heathen nations were to be won, and they, like the Jews, needed the Bible. The sacred Book was not a fetich kept in charge by a hierarchy; it was the voice of God speaking in reproof, in instruction, and in upbuilding in righteousness.

Use of the Bible by the laity

The great German critic Harnack has triumphantly proved by an examination of the writings of the church fathers that the Bible was open to all Christians during these early centuries. More than that, the duty of daily Bible reading was enjoined upon all, catechumens and mature Christians alike; and the practice of a daily "*lectio*" or Bible reading prevailed in family life. It is amazing, in the light of later prohibitions, to learn that during the whole of the first thousand years of the Christian era no instance is known either of prohibition or restriction of Bible reading.

Church fathers on Bible reading

There is not here space to quote from Clement, Polycarp, Tatian, Justin Martyr, and other early church fathers, but it is worthy of note that three of them say that they themselves became Christians through the reading of the Holy Scriptures. Harnack shows that during the period from Irenaeus to Eusebius, while the church fathers were formulating church discipline in regard to baptism and the Lord's supper, no one ever thought of withdrawing the free use of the Scriptures from the laity, but, on the contrary, bishops and teachers united in urging the industrious reading of the Scriptures. Irenaeus says that the Holy Scriptures must, as far as possible, be read by each for himself. Clement writes that married people should pray and read the Scriptures together. He also says that the best time for Bible reading is before the chief meal of the day. The deepest reason for the reading of the Scriptures is that given by Cyprian. "In prayer," he says, "we speak to God, but in reading the Scriptures he speaks to us." Origen considers one or two hours daily not too long a time to devote to divine things. He tells us that his father had made a special point of seeing that his son was instructed in the Scriptures and made him each day learn by heart and repeat some passage.

Children trained in the Scriptures It brings these far-away Christians very close to us when we find instructions that "children in Christian homes should be introduced to the Bible from the very earliest age." "Little boys and girls should learn to put together Biblical names with their ivory letter-blocks, choosing the names from our Lord's genealogies." "Little girls from seven years onward should learn the Psalms by heart and should have read the Bible through before the age of maturity." "We have here," says Harnack, "a glimpse into the home of an ordinary Christian citizen; the children daily hear the Scriptures read and learn passages" of them by heart; a Bible was not only in the home; the Bible was the principal text-book of education; the chief aim in the whole training of a child was that he should be taught to understand the Bible. It was no accident that such use of the Bible made a missionary church and created the need of the first great translations.

Translations by the Greek church The Eastern or Greek church was especially active in this work of translation. To the labors of its earliest missionaries are due the translation into the vernacular tongue of Egypt, the Coptic version; the Syriac version, notably that known as the Peshito; and the Ethiopic or Abyssinian version. The limits of our study do not permit a detailed account of these ancient versions. The Coptic Bible is still used in the worship of the Coptic churches of Egypt, an ancient church long moribund, but now, under the stimulating contact with the American Mission, rising to new life.

The Syriac version The Syriac version exerted a widespread and commanding influence for centuries. The churches of Syria, Armenia, Persia, and Mesopotamia sent their missionaries far into the east and south, carrying the Bible with them. Monuments of this early missionary expansion still exist. In southern India there is a large body of Christians known as the Syrian Christians, which has maintained an unbroken existence from the earliest years of the Christian era. These Syrian Christians in Travancore and Cochin claim that the Apostle Thomas himself was the founder of their church. Whatever be the truth of this tradition it seems certain that early in the fourth century a bishop from Edessa, with a large following of those who were driven out from the Persian Empire during the severe and long-continued persecutions of the Christians, came into India.

Syrian Christians of South India

During the time when Portugal dominated South India these Indian Christians suffered persecution to force them to submit to the church of Rome. These persecutions ceased only with the coming of Dutch and, later, British rule. There are today two bodies of these Syrian Christians, the Roman Catholic numbering about 300,000, and the Syrian Christians proper, not quite so many. These last are undergoing a wonderful awakening, sending their sons to modern schools, overcoming ancient sectarian prejudices and taking on a new sense of responsibility for Christianizing the communities in which they dwell.

The Nestorian Tablet

A monument to the far-flung mission line of the ancient Nestorian Church was disclosed in the discovery of the Nestorian Tablet at Si-nan-fu in northwestern China. It was in 1625 that a Chinese laborer, digging the foundations of a house, unearthed a great slab, seven and one-half feet high by three feet wide. This was covered with Chinese characters surrounded by others which the Chinese could not decipher. It was in a state of perfect preservation. Jesuit missionaries made known the discovery of this treasure, but no attention was paid to it. Semedo, the priest who reported the discovery, was later transferred to South India, where he learned that the strange characters were undoubtedly Syriac. The Nestorian Tablet continued to excite discussion and for the most part derision (Voltaire scoffed at the idea of its authenticity) until 1853, when the American Oriental Society, on the instigation of an American missionary, Dr. E. C. Bridgman, began a scientific investigation. A great sinologue, Mr. A. Wylie, made the investigation, found the tablet, took a rubbing of it and published his translation. His findings and translation were confirmed by later visitors before the precious monument was broken and partially defaced by vandals. The tablet contains an edict by a Chinese emperor in 746 A.D. It eulogizes Christianity, gives a brief summary of Christian doctrine, speaks of twenty-seven sacred books (the New Testament), of baptism, and of the Trinity. It further recounts the arrival of the missionaries in 635 A.D. and commends the new faith. The square border contains lists of the names of the priests and officials.

Monuments of Syrian missions This ancient monument in China and the three Persian crosses with their old Syriac inscriptions found during some excavations near Madras, South India, are the permanent witnesses to the missionary activities of these Syrian Christians. The inscription about the cross in the India tablet reads: "*Let me not glory except in the cross of our Lord Jesus Christ.*"

The Vulgate of St. Jerome The greatest translation of the Bible during the early centuries of Christianity was that by St. Jerome into Latin, commonly called the Vulgate. This great version displaced earlier and crude Latin translations and became the authoritative Bible of the Roman church. As the Eastern empire broke up and the use of Greek declined, the Vulgate became the only Bible generally accessible in Europe during the Middle Ages. The Vulgate, indeed, was the text from which the first great English translation, that of Wyclif, was made.

The Bible of Ulfias, the Goth Before we leave the subject of these early translations one more must be mentioned, that of Ulfilas into Gothic during the middle of the fourth century, in order to give the gospel to the barbarian tribes who were continually pressing down upon the old Roman Empire from the north. The civilization of the Roman Empire was saved from complete destruction at the hands of the barbarians, because these conquering hordes had been in part already redeemed from barbarism by the missionaries of the cross. Among the greatest of these was Ulfilas, who for the love of Christ and his gospel left the city of Constantinople and "all its luxuries" to bury himself among the Goths in the dark forest, beyond the Danube. Before he died in 381 A.D., Ulfilas saw practically the whole Gothic nation following in the footsteps of their King Athanaric in the profession of the Christian faith. The Goths had no written language. Ulfilas invented one, borrowing some of his letters from Latin and Greek. They had no books. He translated the Bible for them, and it was circulated in manuscript among their roving tribes as their chief treasure. "We know," says Gibbon, "that the Goths and Vandals alike carried it with them on their wanderings through Europe. The Vandals took it into Spain and Africa and with their leader Genseric it came round to Rome." A fragment of this earliest writing in Germanic speech has been preserved for us and is now cherished in the library of the University of Upsala, Sweden. The manuscript is written in letters of silver on purple vellum. Other fragments of the Bible of Ulfilas have been recovered from various monasteries.

Decline of Bible reading and revival in the 11C

During the break-up of the Roman Empire the number of schools and readers declined, and the church steadily advanced in its hierarchical and liturgical features. It gradually came about that only the "religious," that is, those in monasteries or the priesthood, were expected to read the Scriptures. It was felt to be inexpedient to translate the Holy Writings into the crude new vernaculars of the people. Most people were illiterate and did not want the Bible, because they could not read it. But in the eleventh century, with the awakening of civilization, reading again became popular and the people suddenly began to want to read the Bible. The church, fearful of heresy, opposed the idea of lay-reading of the Bible; but the idea would not [hold] down. In various parts of Europe different men began the attempt to translate the Bible into the mother tongue of the common people, undeterred by the fact that such attempts were sternly suppressed and often resulted in the imprisonment or execution of the translator.

The English Bible

The greatest among all the European translations are the English and German. Wyclif, Tyndale, Coverdale, and the later translators made the Christian Scriptures accessible to the common people of England, in a translation that is acknowledged to be the greatest literary masterpiece of the English language. The circulation and influence of Wyclif's version is shown by the fact that, although every copy that could be found was burned, one hundred and seventy copies are still preserved. Lord Bacon tells us that at the time of Queen Elizabeth's coronation, when the petitions for the release of political prisoners were presented to Her Majesty, one of her courtiers told her that there were five other prisoners long and unjustly detained in prison. When asked to name them the petitioner replied that they were the four evangelists and the Apostle Paul, who had long been shut up in an unknown tongue, so that they could not converse with the common people.

Bible best adapted to translation

Our main business in this chapter is to trace the work of Bible translation in the modern missionary movement. The phenomenon of Bible translation is without parallel in vastness and variety. No book was ever translated so often or into so many languages. No book ever stood the test of translation so triumphantly. The

Bible neither shrinks nor fades in the process of translation. Just the opposite is true of many of the sacred books. The Koran, for example, from the sonorous beauty of its Arabic style retains its charm for the Moslem mind,—but translate it! Of the result Carlyle says: "A wearisome, confused jumble, crude, incondite; endless iterations, long-windedness, entanglement, insupportable stupidity, in short." John Ruskin says: "I have read three or four pages of the translation of the Koran, and never want to read more."

Bible translations of the last century

At the beginning of the modern era of missions, the Bible had been translated into twenty-eight languages. Since the opening of the nineteenth century the Bible has been translated in whole or in part into four hundred fifty-six languages; the complete Bible into one hundred and twelve languages, the New Testament into one hundred and eleven more languages, and one or more books of Scripture into two hundred and thirty-three other languages. Taking all agencies into account the Bible, in whole or in part, has now been translated into six hundred distinct forms of human speech. There are still languages and dialects, spoken by people, into which the Bible has not yet gone. These are for the most part the languages not yet reduced to writing. In translating the Bible the missionaries have often needed to create an alphabet and written form for the spoken words. They have discovered to the people the capacity of their own tongue.

Translations of Bible vs. those of other books

When the vast work of Bible translation is compared with the translation of other great works of literature, its unique position becomes evident.

The Pilgrim's Progress

The book that stands next to the Bible in the number of its translations is *The Pilgrim's Progress,* which has been put into a hundred languages.

Bible translation essential to missionary progress

The value of this network of Bible translation spread over the whole world can hardly be overestimated. The problem of creating a self-sustaining, self-propagating church in a non-Christian country seems bound up with the supplying of the Bible in the mother tongue and with making it accessible to the ordinary individual. In the ancient missionary enterprises of the church this was not done. The Syrian church made no translations, but took its Syriac Bible into India and China. The Roman Catholic missionaries were for the most part content to allow the gospel to remain wrapped in its Latin vestments.

The heroic Jesuit missionaries who endeavored to win the North American Indians to Christ left no permanent impress, as they left no Gospels. Their great work in Japan was the more easily stamped out by the persecutions of the seventeenth century because the hundreds of thousands of Japanese Christians had no Japanese Bible on which to nourish their faith. On the other hand, the newly evangelized Christians of Madagascar lived through twenty-five years of the most awful persecution, increasing meanwhile from a handful to thousands, because they had the Bible in their possession.

Difficulties of Bible translation

The difficulties of translating the Bible are enormous. In addition to those that inhere in any work of translation there are special difficulties due to the Bible's elevation of thought, and to the extremely backward condition of many of the peoples into whose language the Bible has been translated. There is the difficulty of terminology. How [to] express abstract ideas like sanctification, justification, salvation, retribution, faith, in the language of barbarians or savages? In Tahitan there was no word for *faith* or *conscience*, in the Maori tongue no word for *hope* or *law*. Yet these difficulties have been overcome. The stories of a missionary's search for a word often cover months or even years in which he has been trying to explain the idea to the natives. They have assured him that they had no word to express such an idea, and then some day a word used in a more limited way proves just the one sought for.

Hunting for "thanksgiving"

Among the Kele people in the Congo, Mr. Millman of the English Baptist Missionary Society had long sought the words for *thanks*, *thankfulness*, *thanksgiving*, but without success. One day he killed a leopard which had the day before attempted to carry off a poor woman's little daughter. The mother, leading a band of women, came to his house to sing her gratitude. The first word of her song was *Kelekele*. In telling the story later one of the school boys said, "She gave the white man *kelekele*." Here was the word out of which Mr. Millman could make the various forms to indicate the idea of "thanks" in his translation of the Bible.

Where there are no sheep or shepherds

When the Moravian missionaries in New Guinea translated the Lord's Prayer they had to substitute "Come, thou chieftain great" for "thy kingdom come." In Alaska, where there are no sheep nor shepherds, the missionaries rendered the opening words of the twenty-third Psalm by "The Lord is a first class mountain hunter." In Greenland, John's words, "Behold the Lamb of God," had to be rendered by substituting the name of the only animal about which the people had thoughts of tenderness, "Look God's little seal!"

Enlarging a people's soul

Imagine the difficulties of a translator who tries to phrase "the shadow of a great rock" in the language of Pacific Islanders who have never seen a rock, or to translate "hoar frost," "ice," "snow," for the natives of equatorial Africa, or the "Rose of Sharon and the Lily of the Valley" for the inhabitants of the frozen north. Think of tribes who have no word for *conscience* or *chastity* or *virginity*, and see by what discipline the translated Bible enlarges the soul of a people.

Difficulties in the translator's heart

Nor are the difficulties of translation all exterior to the translators. The greatest assets are in their soul and mind; in their grasp on the truth, their knowledge of the new language; their appreciation of delicate distinctions of meaning; their ability to orientalize themselves so as to "think black" with the African, or think Chinese with the Chinese; their willingness to lay aside prejudice and preconception so that the Book may flow through their minds unwarped and uncolored by sectarian or theological twists of their own; their pluck and endurance and unwearied patience. All these enter into the making of a translation and make its excellence. It is the fight in their own soul that is the real battle ground in translation.

Benefits of Bible translation

The difficulties attending the translation of the Bible sink into insignificance when we contrast them with the benefits which the translators have conferred upon humanity.

Without their aid the modern science of philology could heardly have been created. No motive less compelling than that which drives the missionary to live in desert and savage regions of the earth could have induced scientists to bury themselves for a lifetime in intimate daily association with degraded or savage peoples. The desire to reduce a "language of clicks and grunts and squeaks and hiccoughs" to writing is hardly strong enough to compel the necessary sacrifice. From the days when Ulfilas reduced to writing the language of the Goths and gave them their Bible, and Cyril and Methodius invented an alphabet for the Slavic peoples, and translated the Scriptures into their language until the present time, philological studies have been based largely upon materials supplied by missionary translators. It is necessary to mention only Carey's Sanskrit studies and his polyglot attainments in the languages of India, Koelle who compared one hundred African languages and dialects in his book *Polyglotta Africana* and for these studies was awarded the Volney Prize in 1853 by the French Institute, Mr. J. T. Last of the Church Missionary Society and Rev. W. H. Stapleton of the English Baptist Mission who have greatly furthered the scientific study and classification of the languages of the Congo tribes.

The science of lexicography is equally indebted to these missionary translators. In order to make Bibles they have needed to make dictionaries. These dictionaries have been indispensable to the diplomacy and commerce of Western nations with the Orient. To mention but a few: there is the astounding Dictionary of all Sanskrit-derived languages made by William Carey and destroyed by fire in the printing house of Serampore; there is the same missionary's three-volume Bengali dictionary; there are Judson's monumental Burmese dictionary, Morrison's Chinese dictionary, published by the East India Company at an expense of $60,000, and the later work of S. Wells Williams. These books have laid the whole modern world in debt to their authors. Hepburn's dictionary of Japanese opened an era of contact between Japan and outside nations. The German-Tibetan and the English-Tibetan dictionaries are both the work of one Moravian missionary, Rev. H. A. Jäschke. James S. Dennis, in his *Christian Missions and Social Progress*, vol. III, pp. 409–20, lists sixty-one dictionaries of different African languages, among them the monumental dictionary of the Kaffir language in five hundred octavo pages, double columns, which occupied well-nigh the whole lifetime of Albert Krapf. There are thirty-seven dictionaries in the tongues of British India, among them the Tamil-English dictionary of Dr. Miron Winslow, consisting of 67,452 words; of these 30,551 were listed for the first time by this missionary lexicographer. The various dialects of China are served by twenty-one dictionaries.

William Carey, translator of the Book

The life stories of these missionary translators are of surpassing interest. Prominent among them all is William Carey, a man worthy to stand among the few most highly endowed men of all time. His life is too well known to need retelling but many who are familiar with his services as a great missionary pioneer do not realize his superb gifts as a linguist.

Extent of his labors

Carey made or edited, between the years 1801 and 1822, thirty-six translations of the Scriptures; six were versions of the entire Bible, and twenty-three, of the entire New Testament. Not only were these translations made, but they were published, every step of the mechanical process being attended with incredible toil. When the traveler looks upon that row of ponderous tomes preserved in the library of the college founded by Carey at Serampore, and realizes that these and more are the product of one person's labors, or of his revision and direction of other men's work, the achievement seems superhuman. In addition to these thirty-six translations Carey edited and printed eight other versions for whose translating he was not responsible. It is not to be forgotten that he himself had to break ground, being for the most part without lexicons, grammars, and commentaries. Says Henry C. Vedder:

> The mythical labors of Hercules are a feather-weight compared to Carey's actual labors. Well does he deserve the title that has been bestowed upon him, the Wyclif of India. Before he died, through his agency the Scriptures had been given in their own language to three hundred and thirty million people, one-third of the entire population of the globe; and two hundred and twelve thousand copies of these versions had been issued from the Serampore presses. Surely, it has been seldom given to any man to do a greater work than this, one more far-reaching in its consequences, more lasting in its results.

Adoniram Judson, his sufferings for Burma

Adoniram Judson of Burma is another of the noble army of translators whose exploits are part of the imperishable glory of the Christian Expeditionary Forces. In one respect, that of his sufferings for Christ, it is doubtful whether any other missionary since Paul has surpassed Judson.

Burma was at that time an independent kingdom under the rule of a debased and despotic government. When war broke out between England and Burma, Judson was seized and thrown into the death prison.

The Book in a pillow

In order to protect the precious manuscript of the portion of Dr. Judson's translation of the Bible already completed, Mrs. Judson had hidden it in a pillow which she sewed up in a stout pillowcase and took to her husband for his comfort in his imprisonment. When the prisoners were suddenly removed from Ava to Aungbinle, the pillow was carelessly thrown out into the yard. From here it was rescued by a faithful servant, who kept it hidden until the war was over and he could restore it to the Judsons. Thus were the precious pages, the work of years, preserved.

Judson's task completed

It was twenty-one years before Adoniram Judson finished his translation of the entire Bible into Burmese. His fine scholarship, refusal to be satisfied with anything short of the best possible Burmese phrase, and unremitting toil combined to make this Burmese translation basic for any later work of revision, as Luther's Bible in German, and Tyndale's translation in English are basic.

Importance of translating Bible into Chinese

A major strategic operation in Christianity's conquest of the world was the translation of the Bible into Chinese, the language of one-fourth of the human race. To make the Christian message available to such a fraction is by virtue of its very vastness, an outstanding fact in the story of human progress; but where the achievement is weighed as well as surveyed, its true importance appears.

Robert Morrison, master workman

As ever in any great enterprise, there is in this enterprise of translating the Bible into Chinese one outstanding man, Robert Morrison of England. In his early adulthood he had dedicated himself to the work of Christ. He wrote:

> Jesus, I have given myself to thy service. The question with me is, where shall I serve? I learn from thy Word that it is thy holy pleasure that the Gospel should be preached in all the world, for a witness to all nations. . . . When I view the field, O Lord, my Master, I perceive that by far the greater part is entirely without laborers . . . whilst there are thousands crowded up in one corner. My desire is, O Lord, to engage where laborers are most wanted.

God granted him his desire and sent him to China, where he worked faithfully against terrible obstacles to give the gospel to the Chinese. Since all public presentation of Christianity was forbidden, he saw that his one line of access lay in the preparing of books. He gave his remarkable powers to the study of Chinese. He prepared a grammar and an Anglo-Chinese dictionary. After sixteen years he published his dictionary, containing forty thousand words. In its preparation he had consulted ten thousand Chinese volumes, and gained a knowledge of Chinese writings such as no European had ever possessed. The East India Company published the dictionary in six huge volumes, at a cost of $60,000.

God's providential preparation

God had been the great pioneer, as he always is in making paths in the desert along which the human pioneer may find his way. An unknown Catholic missionary had completed a translation of part of the New Testament—Acts, Luke, and some of the Epistles—and his forgotten manuscript was discovered by Morrison in the British Museum. A Chinese man was found living in London, at that time a very unusual circumstance. This man guided Morrison in his first explorations of the language, and taught him how to use a Chinese camel's hair brush in writing Chinese characters. With the help which this man could give him, Morrison began, and in a few months completed transcriptions of this manuscript copy of the New Testament. He took this book with him to China, and also a copy of a Latin-Chinese vocabulary which he had made in the same laborious manner. While very imperfect, these both proved valuable to him in unlocking the mysteries of the language.

Publishing an distributing first Chinese Bibles

The salary received by Morrison from the East India Company for his services as translator enabled him to carry on his ceaseless studies in the preparation of a Bible for the Chinese. He was joined in these labors by Robert Milne, who worked with him with one heart and soul in the great enterprise. The Gospel of Luke was published in 1813, the New Testament in 1814, and the entire Bible in 1819. The death penalty was still in force against any Chinese who adopted a foreign religion, and so Morrison and Milne were forced to distribute their Bibles for the most part among the Chinese who had emigrated from their own land and were both more liberal and more accessible. They were distributed in the Chinese colonies in Java, Molucca, and Penang. An indication of the difficulties of Bible distribution in those days is given in a report written in 1822, in which it is recorded as "a matter for profound gratitude to God that during the year five hundred copies of the New Testament and some books of the Old Testament had been put into circulation, although it was still impracticable to distribute the Sacred Volume within the domains of the Emperor of China." At that time and for many years later all these books had to be given away. It was impossible to sell them.

Later translators: Schereschewsky

The field of Bible translation in China is a fascinating one. Its extent may be realized by perusing a pamphlet of thirty-nine pages published by the American Bible Society in 1916. The entire pamphlet is simply a list of the various translations and revisions made up to that time. It is possible to mention but a few of the many men and women who have toiled to give the Word of God to the Chinese. Among the most picturesque characters is Bishop Schereschewsky (pronounced Skĕr-ĕs-kūs'ky) of the Protestant Episcopal church. He was a Russian Jew, born in 1831. He was converted in Holland through reading the New Testament. He received his theological education in America, whence he was sent to China as a missionary of the Protestant Episcopal church. Bishop Schereschewsky became one of the great translators. He had part in the revision of the Mandarin Bible and made a translation of the entire Bible into the Wenli or classical Chinese. During many years of his life he was bedridden and paralyzed, having only partial use of one hand, but he completed his task. Among other translators are Gützlaff, who made the version used by the leaders of the Tai Ping rebellion, Rev. William Dean, W. A. P. Martin, Rev. Griffith John, Rev. C. W. Mateer, and Rev. Chauncey Goodrich.

A Japanese Bible made in China

The Bible played a great part in the opening of Japan to the gospel. Here again Providential preparation is seen. Dr. Karl Friedrich August Gützlaff was another of the linguistic giants whom God had endowed and brought into the world to make the Bible known outside the bounds of Christendom. Dr. Gützlaff had been sent to the Far East in 1828 by the Netherlands Missionary Society. On his way to his field in China he was detained in Siam and improved his time by translating the Bible into Siamese. He reached China in 1831, the very year in which a Japanese junk was storm driven on the Pacific Ocean. The boat, after being tossed about for months, was wrecked on the Oregon coast, the survivors were made slaves by the Indians, rescued by the Hudson Bay Company, and were sent across Canada to England. From London they were sent back to China, and after four years of wandering landed at Macao in December of 1835. Gützlaff took them to his own home, and, not satisfied with having made a beginning in the languages of Siam and China, promptly began to learn Japanese from his guests. In two years he had translated the Gospel and Epistles of John into Japanese, and had them printed at Singapore. It may not be without interest to mention that this same Dr. Gützlaff was the one whose pamphlet on medical missions made Livingstone decide to be a medical missionary, whose Chinese translation of the Bible was republished by the leaders of the Tai Ping rebellion, and who was the author of sixty-one volumes in Chinese.

Versions of S. Wells Williams

At about the same time that Dr. Gützlaff was preparing his Japanese version of the Bible, another group of shipwrecked sailors had been returned by Americans. These may have been driven by the same storm that wrecked the other Japanese junk. They were rescued by some Christian men and sent to China, since the laws of Japan did not permit their return to their own country. Dr. S. Wells Williams, one of the most remarkable men whom America has sent to the East, received and befriended them. Not content with his mastery of the Chinese language—an achievement quite sufficient for one person—he began to learn Japanese from these waifs, and made a translation of the Gospel of Matthew and the book of Genesis. While the Japanese of these sailors was probably none of the purest, Dr. Williams was able to get a sufficient grasp on the language so that he accompanied Commodore Perry as interpreter when the American Navy succeeded in opening Japan to intercourse with the Western world. In 1837 he had tried to gain access to Japan, only to be driven away by the batteries in Yeddo Bay.

The first Protestant missionaries

It was not until 1859 that the first Protestant missionaries entered the newly opened empire of Japan. One of their first tasks was to translate the Bible, since they were still strictly forbidden to do open or aggressive Christian work. During these perilous times the early missionaries devoted themselves to language study and to translation. The five men who reached Japan during the first year of Protestant missions were Rev. John Liggins and Rev., afterward bishop, C. M. Williams of the Protestant Episcopal church, Dr. J. C. Hepburn of the Presbyterian church, and Dr. S. R. Brown and Rev. G. T. Verbeck of the Dutch Reformed. For nearly ten years these men practically had the field to themselves. All were mighty men of God. Quite unexpectedly to Mr. Liggins and Mr. Williams, who had been transferred from China, a demand sprang up for the Bible in Chinese translation. Since the Chinese and Japanese use the same characters (the Chinese) in their writing, the Japanese could understand the Chinese character, although reading it in Japanese words. This may be illustrated by the fact that the French and English both understand Arabic numerals though they give them different names.

A Bible floating on the water

Some Chinese books had a big influence in the introduction of the Japanese to Christianity. In 1855 a young nobleman named Murata Wasaka was in charge of the western coast near Nagasaki, to keep out all foreigners. He kept the harbor guarded by a cordon of boats. One day while on a trip of inspection he found a book floating on the water. The type and binding so interested him, that he picked it out of the water. He asked a Dutch interpreter about the book and was told that it was a New Testament in Dutch, but that there was a translation of it in Chinese. Wasaka sent a man to Shanghai to buy a copy, and began in secret to study its pages with his younger brother and two friends.

Murata and his brother question Verbeck

When the first missionaries arrived these young men were still engaged in the perilous study of the forbidden faith. In 1862 the younger brother, Ayabe, traveled to Nagasaki under pretense of studying medicine but really to try to find some foreigner who could explain passages which were hard to understand. One of his questions was whether Jesus was an Englishman, a Dutchman, or a Spaniard. Here he formed the acquaintance of Guido Verbeck and warned him of a plot against his life. From time to time the two brothers, with elaborate precautions against discovery, sent a trusted servant named Motono with new lists of questions. At that time there were no railroads and the journey to Nagasaki took two days. Verbeck prepared a page of home helps for these young men every week. Finally the two brothers, with no witness except their trusted servant, were baptized, and Motono also, by Dr. Verbeck in the springtime of 1866. With great courage both brothers reported their act to their feudal lord. Neither of them suffered persecution, though some of Wasaka's Christian books were burned by order of the central government.

Translators and translations

The Japanese Bible of today is the work of a group of translators, the earliest and greatest of whom were Dr. S. R. Brown, Dr. Hepburn, Dr. Green, and Dr. Nathan Brown. This committee began its work in January 1874 and worked for five years before the first edition was published in April 1880. Dr. Hepburn, one of the most famous of these men, was the maker of the first English-Japanese dictionary. When he went to Japan there were no helps in the study of the language. He had to depend on writing down the sounds of words on tablets as he learned them. He studied with such good purpose that in eight years he was able to publish a superb specimen of lexicography, the English-Japanese dictionary, on which all subsequent dictionaries are based. The completed version of the New Testament was published by the committee in 1880, and that of the entire Bible in 1888. Separate Gospels and portions were put into circulation as soon as they were completed; the Gospel of Mark in 1872 and that of Matthew a year later.

The revision committee and its work The rapid progress of the Japanese language toward standardization, the introduction of new term and the more intimate acquaintance with the language on the part of the missionaries made a revised version seem desirable. A committee composed of Japanese and missionary members was chosen in 1910. Two of its members, Dr. Greene and Mr. Matsuyama, had been members of the original committee; the others, both foreign and Japanese, were all chosen because of their expert knowledge of one or more phases of the work. This revision "is in a modified classical style with archaic forms omitted and the language brought nearer to modern speech," says Dr. C. K. Harrington, one of the translators. Since the difference between the spoken and the written language is immeasurably greater than is the case in any modern Western language, all will echo Dr. Harrington's hope that "some day there may be a translation into the real vernacular, the colloquial."

The Bible finds a prepared path The Christians of Korea are preeminently Bible Christians. The Koreans seem to have had a wonderful preparation for the diffusion of the gospel. Owing to similarities in their life and customs with conditions pictured in the Scripture, it spoke to them from the first as a native and not a foreign book. The people of the Book said, "Peace be with you" in their daily salutations; so did the Koreans. Sacrifices and peace offerings were well known to Koreans; they "went out to meet the bridegroom"; and "two women grinding at the mill" were no strange sight to them. They could pick up their beds and walk; they saw the fishermen mending their nets and the winnowing fans on the threshing floor. They had feasts of the new moon, they wore long robes girt about with a fancy girdle. They put off their shoes when they stood on holy ground. They knew about demons and the demoniacs and the helplessness of the sorcerers to drive out the demons. They had visions and parables and dreams. When the Book came it found its way prepared.

The Korean script They had a wonderful aid, too, in their system of writing their language. The Chinese and Japanese were lumbering along with written characters so complex and difficult as virtually to fence away the domain of literature from the common people. Four hundred and seventy-five years ago (1445 A.D.), Korea prepared a simple form of syllabic alphabet or phonetic writing so that, as Moffatt says, "the old and the poor, the toil-worn, the prisoner, the hidden wife and mother, the slave behind the mule, the butcher, the baker, the hat-mender, the water-carrier, the bean-curd peddler, the sorcerer, the witch-wife, the less than no one, all might read." King Sejong's simple alphabet, so simple that the art of reading might be learned in a few weeks, lay disused and despised for centuries by the Koreans. Chinese characters were used for their classical literature, while their own phonetic writing was called *Un-Mun*, "the dirty language." But when the Lord Jesus must needs go through Korea, he picked the despised alphabet from the dust, saying, "This was made for my gospel." The miraculously rapid circulation of the New Testament was due in no small degree to the fact that it was printed in the native script. May it not be that this translation of the Bible into Korean will prove to be not only the means of preserving the Korean language, but also the model on which both Japan and China may modify their antiquated and complicated system of character writing?

A Korean Bible made in Manchuria

The Bible entered Korea in advance of the missionary, partly because it was easier to smuggle in a Bible than a missionary in the days when signposts along the road said: "If you meet a foreigner, kill him; he who has friendly relations with him is a traitor to his country." These signposts stood as late as 1880. It was in 1865, twenty years before the coming of the missionaries, that the earliest known attempt was made to bring the Bible into Korea. Mr. Thomas, an agent of the National Bible Society of Scotland, came bringing Chinese Bibles from Chefoo in a Korean junk. He knew that since Korean scholars wrote their own language with the Chinese characters they could read this Chinese Bible. A year later he was stranded in the ill-fated Sherman and both he and the crew were killed by the Koreans.

In 1875 Dr. John Ross and Rev. John McIntyre of the United Presbyterian church of Scotland, working in Manchuria, made the acquaintance of Koreans who had gone to Manchuria on business. They found out that the Koreans could understand the Chinese Bible, since they read their own language in Chinese characters. A scholarly Korean was engaged to make a translation from the Chinese into the *Un-Mun,* the vernacular writing of Korea. In 1882 translations of the Gospels of St. Luke and St. John had been made and published. Work done by such an agent under such conditions was bound to prove imperfect; but it surely was under the direction of the Great

Strategist that these two missionaries in Manchuria were led to adopt the Korean rather than the Chinese script for their first translation.

Colporters smuggle it into Korea

Once printed it looked hopeless to get the books introduced, since all foreign religious books were prohibited in the Hermit Kingdom. It was finally decided to make the Scriptures up into bundles, unbound, and send them in on the backs of the coolies who carried great bundles of old official papers bought up annually in Manchuria by Korean merchants. The plan succeeded. In a short time there was a little company of disciples among the merchants of Weiju in the northern end of the country. Three of these early disciples, at great personal risk, became colporters. One of them, Saw Sang Yun, succeeded in getting to Seoul from Mukden with a few copies of the Scripture. He was in Seoul when the American missionaries came in 1885.

Another translation enters from the East

Meanwhile, another attempt to enter Korea with a Korean Bible had been made in Japan. Rev. Henry Loomis, agent of the American Bible Society in Yokohama, met a Korean and engaged him to translate the Gospel of Mark into Korean. When the pioneer missionaries, Dr. H. G. Underwood, Dr. H. G. Appenzeller, and Dr. W. B. Scranton, passed through Japan in 1885, a few copies of this Gospel of Mark were given to them. It was the Ross translation, however, which was the real forerunner of missions. Between 1883 and 1886 no less than 15,690 copies of this translation had been circulated. Saw Sang Yun had led the first Korean congregation to Christ. To this day the Christian church in Weiju, where no missionary is resident, numbers fifteen hundred believers.

Authorized version of Korean Bible

However valuable these first attempts at translation, the American missionaries realized that another and better translation must be made. A board of translators was formed in 1887. An authorized version of the New Testament was completed and published in 1906, six years after a tentative version had been put in circulation. It was not until 1910 that the translation of all the books of the Old Testament was completed.

The Bible among the islanders

Some of the great adventures in Bible translation belong to the little peoples. The Gilbert Islanders, for example, clinging to their low-lying coral reefs, had the lifetime of a Christian hero given in their behalf, in the endeavor to give them the Bible.

Hiram Bingham Jr., son of that Hiram Bingham who brought the gospel to the Hawaiian Islanders, lived on the Gilbert Islands, reduced the language to writing, made a grammar and dictionary, and after years of toil translated the Bible. His manuscript, the fruit of a lifetime, was lost at sea on its way to America to be published. Although his health was shattered so that he could no longer continue to live in the Gilbert Islands, Mr. Bingham while living in Hawaii, patiently renewed his labors to retranslate the whole. On all the Pacific Islands there are similar stories of peoples sunk in degradation, and of the coming of the missionaries bringing the Book. It was in Aneityum, one of the islands of the New Hebrides, that John Geddie of Nova Scotia began in 1848 to learn the language of the fierce savages who inhabited the island. He reduced their language to writing, prepared school books, taught the people to read, translated the Bible for them. When he died, worn out after twenty-four years of service, a bronze tablet was placed in his memory in a church seating one thousand worshippers:

> When he landed in 1848, there were no Christians here;
> When he left in 1872, there were no heathen.

The people were so overjoyed at the thought of having the Bible in their own tongue that they contributed $5,000 for printing it. These same islanders gave the entire product of their cocoanut trees for six months to roof two churches, and sent out and paid more than fifty of their own members who went carrying their Bible as missionaries to heathen islands.

Henry Nott of Tahiti

One of the master translators of the South Sea Islands was Henry Nott of Tahiti. He gave twenty years of his life, amid circumstances full of horror and suffering, to the study of the language. He tamed it, cleared out its dense thickets of savage thought, discovered its hidden symmetries and beauties, and after he felt himself master gave another twenty years of a great life to the translation of the Scriptures.

John Williams of Raratonga

When John Williams later began his cruises of Christianization, he translated the New Testament into Raratongan, a closely allied dialect. He spent four years in England perfecting his translation and seeing it through the press. When he returned to Raratonga with his big boxes of books,—five thousand of them,—the people crowded around to secure the priceless treasures. "Every one was eager to buy a copy," John Williams says, "One man, as he secured his, hugged the book in ecstasy; another and another kissed it; others held them up and waved them in the air. Some sprang away like a dart, and did not stop till they entered their own dwellings, and exhibited their treasures to their wives and children, while others jumped and capered about like persons half frantic with joy."

John G. Paton of Aniwa

John G. Paton, translator of the New Testament into Aniwan, one of the many languages of the New Hebrides, tells of the joy which the first book gave to the Chief Namekei; "Is it done? Can it speak?" asked Namekei excitedly. "Make it speak to me! Let me hear it speak." When part of the book was read to him he shouted in an ecstasy of joy, "It does speak! It speaks my own language, too! Oh, give it to me!" He grasped it hurriedly, opened and then closed it with a look of disappointment, and said, "I can not make it speak! It will never speak to me." But it did, for the old Chief with painful persistence learned to read, and as children and strangers gathered round him he would produce his prized book and say, "Come, I will let you hear how the book speaks our own Aniwan words."

The Bible in Savage Island and New Guinea

Time would fail to tell of two brothers, W. G. Lawes and F. E. Lawes, who gave thirty-six years of their lives to clear a path for the Book into the minds of the men of Savage Island; or of the seven years given by this same W. G. Lawes to complete and revise the New Testament translated by James Chalmers into the speech of one of the tribes of New Guinea, for men of the Stone Age.

Searching for a name for God

The translator of the New Testament into Toaripi, one of the languages spoken in southern New Guinea, Rev. E. Pryce Jones, tells of the difficulty he had to find a word for *God* that would convey the Christian idea to people still in the stage of totem worship. He could find the names of the different spirits who made the pig, the crocodile, or the crab, but all his searching failed to find any higher idea. One day when he was working with a native and asking him questions the man said,

"Ualare knows that."

"Who is Ualare?" asked the missionary quickly, hoping that perhaps he was at last on the trail.

"Ualare is the spirit who made the mountains, and out of whom the world came," said the man.

Today the Papuan reads in his New Testament, "Ualare so loved the world that he gave his only begotten Son," and slowly builds up his idea of a great Father God.

Christianity comes to Madagascar

The island of Madagascar, on the other side of the world from these small, smiling lands circled about with silver seas, has been the scene of one of the greatest victories of the Bible translator. Madagascar is next to New Guinea the largest island in the world. Between four and five million people live on this rich island. They built comfortable homes, were decently clad, often in garments made of the silk they spun and wove so cunningly. They spun cotton, too, and hemp, and knew how to work iron so as to make their spears and spades. Some of their towns were surrounded by walls and moats. Their government was an absolute despotism. The slave trade cursed them. Although having considerable beginnings of civilization, they had no written language and their moral condition was exceedingly low. In 1818 the London Missionary Society sent two missionaries and their families. In six weeks all except one, Rev. David Jones, were dead. He escaped to Mauritius, tortured with fever. In 1820 he reentered the country; other missionaries joined him, and the task of hewing out a vocabulary and grammar of the language began. Schools were opened. King Radama sent ten picked youths to England to be educated. The schools in Madagascar grew mightily. In 1828 the Gospel of Luke was published. In that same year the wise king died and a reign of terror ensued, set up by rival claimants to the throne. All schools were closed, so that the missionaries were shut up to the one work of Bible translation. The printing press had already been set up by the missionaries. By 1830 five thousand copies of the complete New Testament were printed. Then came edicts allowing the reopening of the schools, and the very next year the first converts were baptized and the church began to grow in apostolic fashion.

Ranavalona begins the great persecution

Then began the opposition which later was to develop into ruthless persecution. Ranavalona, the queen, became the bitter enemy of the new religion. On March first, 1835, a decree went forth that all who met for prayer and worship must confess it within a month. In swift succession came decrees ordering the giving up and burning of all copies of the Scriptures. The missionaries were then driven out and the full fury of the storm broke on the infant church. The missionaries, before going, buried their boxes of Bibles, Testaments, and *The Pilgrim's Progress*, to await their return and the dawn of better days. Well that they did not dream that twenty-six years were to pass before the mission stations could again be opened. During that time no devilish refinement of torture was missing in the sufferings meted out to the Malagasy Christians. The only legacy which the missionaries had been able to leave to their sorely tried converts was the books which they had printed. Since these books were the only ones in the language, they had been read without distraction by all classes of the people. On the New Testament and *The Pilgrim's Progress*, the Christians were to feed their souls during the black years of persecution that followed.

Another eleventh chapter of Hebrews

There are no more glorious annals in the history of Christianity than those of Madagascar. All the Bibles which could be found were burned, but copies were secreted in hollow trees, in caves, in the rafters of houses. Rough copies were made by hand and passed secretly from disciple to disciple. When the years of agony were over, some of these precious tear-stained, bloodstained copies, worn thin from much handling, mended again and again, were recovered, and may now be seen in the archives of the British and Foreign Bible Society. Those who refused to worship the idols and boldly confessed their belief in Christ were sold as slaves, forced to toil in chains, driven out into the forests, thrown over cliffs into the sea, suspended head downward in the rice pits and boiling water poured over them, burned alive, dismembered. Nobles saw their families scattered and reduced to slavery, their estates confiscated, themselves reduced to the ranks of the common soldiers and put to hard labor. This went on for year after year, yet still the faith grew and spread, irresistible, unquenchable.

End of reign of terror

When the reign of terror had ended and the first consignment of Bibles, long stored in Mauritius in anticipation of the day of the gospel's reentrance, arrived at the capital, so vast a crowd pressed forward to buy the books that the doors of the storehouse had to be closed, a line formed, and the Bibles passed out through the window to the waiting purchasers.

The Book that sets men free

What shall we say of a Book that can beget such heroism? Does it need other credentials that it is God's best gift to humanity? When the missionaries had been driven out, there were about fifteen hundred Christians. When they were allowed to return, there were seven thousand. During the twenty-six years ten thousand people had been sentenced to death or slavery or exile. What was the power which had sustained these new believers, fresh from heathen and debasing customs? The Book whose mere introduction could arouse such devotion may well be called the Charter of Humanity's Freedom.

The Bible enthroned

In 1868, when Queen Ranavalona II was crowned, the royal seat was erected under a canopy on each side of which was emblazoned a quotation from the Bible: "Glory to God"; "Good will among men"; "On earth peace"; "God be with us." In front of the queen were two tables, on one of them the crown of Madagascar, on the other, the Bible.

The Bible in Africa

The Dark Continent has been the scene of many triumphs of the translator. Africa is the true Tower of Babel. Here are eight hundred and forty-three varieties of human speech, almost all of them to be reduced to written form, most of them spoken by savage tribes living under conditions almost insupportable by white men. Yet into this darkness men have gone, and there they have lived and worked to bring the Book of God to the people. The missionaries have made dictionaries and grammars and school books and translated the Bible into one hundred different languages; but there remain four hundred and forty-three distinct languages and three hundred dialects not yet reduced to writing. If Africa is transferred from a liability into an asset, it will be because the Africans receive the Christian Bible.

Pilkington of Uganda

It will be impossible to mention more than one or two of these translators. George Lawrence Pilkington of Uganda is one of the most gifted in any land. Such was his facility in the acquisition of language that he learned the language on his way up from Zanzibar so that he was able to converse as soon as he reached his field. Within five years after reaching Uganda, Pilkington carried back to his home in Ireland the manuscript of the entire New Testament and a large part of the Old for final revision and printing. Although so rapid, his work was exceedingly careful and scholarly.

Eliot's Bible for the Indians

The story of the Bible among the North American Indians must not be passed over. The first American translation of the Bible was that made by John Eliot in the language of the Mohicans of New England. It was only fifty years after the publication of the King James Version of the English Bible that John Eliot's translation of the New Testament was printed in 1661, and two years later that of the Old Testament. The Indian tribes for whom the Book was translated have long since vanished, their very language is forgotten so that no one living can read one of the cherished copies of the beautifully printed Bible; but Eliot's work remains, as does his word inscribed at the end of his Indian grammar, "Prayer and pains, through faith in Jesus Christ, will do anything." Translations of portions of the Bible were early made into the language of the Delawares, the Mohawks, the Senecas, and the Chippewas.

"The white man's book of heaven" The story of the search for the Bible on the part of the Nez-Perces Indians of Idaho is one of the most stirring in the annals of missions. In their far fastnesses the tribe had heard about a book of heaven through which the white man became wise and strong. In a great council the tribe set apart four chiefs to go to the distant white man's country and bring back the Book. It was in 1831 that these four men made their way over the desolate mountains, the vast prairies, the swift rivers, and came to St. Louis, a rough, roystering frontier town, asking,

"Where is the white man's book of heaven?"

They met ridicule and indifference until General Clark learned of their errand and befriended them. Two of the Indians fell ill and died. Before the others started on their long homeward journey a big dinner was given in their honor, at which the officers at the fort and the leading citizens were present.

The Oregon Trail Although the Indians in far-away Idaho who waited month after month for the return of their emissaries with the Book waited in vain, yet this appeal did reach the hearts of the white people. As a result the first Protestant mission west of the Rocky Mountains was established, Jason Lee of the Methodist Episcopal church becoming the pioneer. Marcus Whitman and Henry H. Spalding, with their brides, began a honeymoon journey lasting seven months to the far Northwest. Greater issues, too, hung upon their mission than the Indian chiefs who made the perilous journey could dream. On the fact that these American missionaries with wagons, household goods, and families had actually crossed the Rocky Mountains depended very largely America's claim to the Oregon country. After long, long delays the Nez-Perces actually got "The Book that makes the trail plain," printed in their own language by the American Bible Society in 1871.

The Dakota Bible The greatest Indian translation is that into the language of the Sioux of the plains, the Dakotas. Two men, Rev. Thomas E. Williamson and Dr. Stephen Riggs, gave forty years of life to this task. Their joint work was revised by Dr. Williamson's son, the Rev. John P. Williamson. Dr. Riggs' autobiography, *Mary and I, or Forty Years among the Sioux*, is a moving and glorious record.

The Nevajo Bible The most recent translation of the Bible into an Indian tongue is the Nevajo. This numerous tribe living in Arizona and New Mexico has waited all these years for the white people to give them the Book. Three men, Rev. L. P. Brink, Rev. F. G. Mitchell, and Rev. John Butler, have collaborated in the work of translation.

An Indian invents an alphabet The Cherokee Scriptures are notable not so much because of the translation as because they are printed in an alphabet invented by a Cherokee Indian, a half-breed, whose Indian name was Sequoya. Although illiterate himself, he realized that the power of the white people was bound up in their books. He studied to see if he could supply the need of his own people. He made symbols on birch bark, and in some way got the idea of making symbols represent the sounds of the Cherokee language. After two years' work he invented an alphabet consisting of eighty-four letters. This alphabet was adopted by the legislature of the Cherokee Nation, and a newspaper was published in it. The missionaries adopted it for the translation of the Bible, as by means of this alphabet it was possible to represent the sounds of the Cherokee language more perfectly than by the English alphabet. In 1831 the American Bible Society began the printing of the Cherokee New Testament and a large part of the Old Testament. The state of Oklahoma has recently presented to the government a statue of Sequoya to be placed in the Capitol at Washington.

The Indian's Twenty-Third Psalm

The Indian language is not easily subject to translation and in their intercourse with one another the various tribes use a sign language, more or less universal, which they have evolved. The following is a translation of the twenty-third Psalm which can easily be interpreted by this sign language:

The Great Father above is a Shepherd Chief. I am His, and with Him I want not.

He throws out to me a rope, and the name of the rope is Love, and He draws me, and He draws me, and He draws me to where the grass is green and the water not dangerous, and I eat and lie down satisfied.

Sometimes my heart is very weak and falls down, but He lifts it up again and draws me into a good road. His name is Wonderful.

Some time, it may be very soon, it may be longer, it may be a long, long time, He will draw me into a place between mountains. It is dark there, but I'll draw back not. I'll be afraid not, for it is in there between these mountains that the Shepherd Chief will meet me, and the hunger I have felt in my heart all through this life will be satisfied. Sometimes He makes the love rope into a whip, but afterwards He gives me a staff to lean on.

He spreads a table before me with all kinds of food. He puts His hands upon my head, and all the "tired" is gone. My cup He fills till it runs over.

What I tell you is true, I lie not. These roads that are "away ahead" will stay with me through this life, and afterward I will go to live in the "Big Tepee" and sit down with the Shepherd Chief forever.

Arabic, sacred language of Moslems

The Bible has been made accessible through translation to Moslem populations numbering 200 million. All of these revere one sacred language, the Arabic, in which the Koran was written by verbal inspiration, as they believe. So great is their reverence for the very word of Scripture that they discourage any translation of the Koran, which is read in its original Arabic wherever there is a Mosque, and forms the basis of education wherever there is a Moslem school. A well-known Moslem lawyer in Lahore, India, in addressing his coreligionists said recently, "The reason why Christians succeed is because wherever they go they have the Bible and say their prayers in their mother tongue; whereas we have wrapped up our religion in an Arabic dress. We ought to give the people the Koran in their own tongue." His only answer was, "Thou art an unbeliever thyself, to say such things."

Translation of Arabic Bible

The importance of an Arabic version of the Bible becomes apparent when we consider the fanatical devotion to Arabic throughout the whole Moslem world scattered over Asia and Africa. This need was met by a wonderful translation into classical Arabic to which Rev. Cornelius VanDyke and Rev. Eli Smith gave sixteen years of life. Their translation ranks among the very greatest in its felicity and strength; its pure Arabic style makes it a delight to the reader of Arabic literature.

Not content with this version in high Arabic, the British and Foreign Bible Society has made translations into the colloquial Arabic spoken in the various countries of the Near East.

Other Moslem versions

The Moslem world devoted to a Book must be won by a greater Book. To the winning of peoples who profess this most powerful religion now opposing Christianity the noble army of translators has contributed much. The Turkish Bible of Schaufer was the work of fourteen years. These two chief versions, the Arabic and the Turkish, are supplemented by ten others in the chief languages of the Levant, and in thirty dialects. Furthermore, the Turkish Bible is printed also in the Arabic, the Armenian, or the Greek characters for those who read Turkish in those alphabets.

A superb achievement

The translation of the Bible has been perhaps the most fruitful accomplishment of the nineteenth century. Until the Scriptures were made accessible to the great bulk of people in their mother tongue, there could be no wide expansion of Christianity. While there are multitudes belonging to the smaller and more scattered peoples who are still without a Bible, the great racial and national divisions have all had the Scriptures translated into their own language. While other faiths have remained more or less quiescent, permitting their sacred books, if translated at all, to be translated by others for the purposes of comparative study of religion, Christians have boldly, persistently, with superb courage and devotion, laid down life itself in the struggle to put the Bible into the speech of every tongue and tribe and nation. The first campaign is won.

Strategy of Bible translation

Into all these lands the Bible has found entrance through the labor of the translators. As battles are won not solely or even chiefly by the armies who struggle with shot and shell in the front line, but by the makers of munitions and by the strategists who, far back, are directing the campaign, so Christianity's world campaign depends upon these missionaries who are translating the Bible into living languages. Wherever it goes the Book carries its credentials. It speaks one message to the one heart of humankind. As a Greek Christian phrased it in his letter to the Bible House, in broken English but no doubtful meaning, "The gabs are many, but the ghost is one."

Outline

Chapter 4

AIM: To show how the work of the National Bible Societies has powerfully furthered the missionary movement by financing translations, and publishing and distributing Bibles.

I. Historical Sketch of the National Bible Societies
   1. The British and Foreign Bible Society
      a. Circumstances surrounding its organization
      b. Its charter, activities, rapid development
   2. Continental Bible Societies
      a. Fostered by British and Foreign Bible Society
      b. Some short-lived
      c. Most of them doing little missionary translation
   3. The National Bible Society of Scotland
   4. The American Bible Society
      a. Its organization
      b. Distinguished support
      c. Bible publication endorsed by Congress

II. Work of the National Bible Societies
   1. Common principles and policies
   2. Selling Bibles or giving them
   3. Promoting and financing of Bible translations and publications

4. Enormous and continuous sale of the Bible
5. Comparison of Bible sales with others

III. The Agent of the Bible Societies
1. The colporter ubiquitous
2. The colporter from every race
3. The colporter of true heroic stuff

IV. The Fruits of Bible Distribution
1. In a Navaho Hogan
2. In a Japansese prison
3. In a Korean prison
4. In Chinese philanthropist
5. In an Indian *fakir*

V. Ministry of the Bible Societies to the Soldiers and Sailors
1. Enormous number distributed; widespread contributions to the fund; approval of military leaders, appreciation of the boys
2. The Pocket Testament League, its story
3. Fruit of Bible work among soldiers

VI. Duties toward the Bible Societies

Four

The Travels of the Book

It is the great destiny of England and America to carry the Bible to the earth's remotest bounds.

Hon. Joseph H. Choate

The rise of Bible societies

In chapter three we have studied the work of Bible translators in aid of the worldwide diffusion of the Christian message. In chapter four we shall consider the history and activities of the great organizations through which the distribution of the manifold translations has been made possible. In reality these two agencies, the translators and the Bible societies, are contemporary with the rise and development of a third agency, the Mission Boards and Societies. It seemed expedient in the interests of clearness to consider them separately.

Bible expensive and scarce in 1800

In the opening years of the nineteenth century Bibles were comparatively few and very expensive. Outside America and the Protestant nations of Europe they were almost unobtainable by the laity. Even in Scotland among the Highlanders, most of whom at that time understood no language but the Gaelic, the scarcity of the Scriptures was extreme. Not only were the books very few and hard to obtain, but the price, twenty-five shillings ($6.25), put them beyond the reach of any except the wealthy. In Ireland, with a population of 5.25 million, there were very few places outside the capital where a Bible could be purchased at any price. In the Island of Jersey old, secondhand family Bibles sold for £4. In the United States an equal destitution existed in the supply of Bibles both among the older settlers and among the pioneers on the frontiers, as was proved by the extensive investigations made by Samuel J. Mills in two journeys taken by him in 1812 and 1813.

Education and invention democratize the Scriptures

The invention of printing had made possible a very great extension in the circulation of the Scriptures, but the full effects of this miracle-working invention waited on two things; the diffusion of popular education and the perfecting of mechanical processes by which the cost of printing was greatly reduced. We do not often consider at how comparatively recent a day the public school system democratized the ability to read, and the power press and other inventions put books within the means of the great mass of people.

What Mary Jones helped to start

It was on March 7, 1804, that the oldest of the National Bible Societies, the British and Foreign Bible Society, was founded at the London Tavern in the presence of about three hundred people. An incident that had been influential in bringing about its founding was the search of a little Welsh girl for a Bible. The Rev. Thomas Charles of Bala had told her story at a meeting of the Committee of the Religious Tract Society one cold December morning in 1802. It seemed that there lived in a valley under Cader Idris, in the parish of Llanfihangel, a young Welsh girl named Mary Jones. She dearly loved the Bible, but the only chance she had to read it was by walking two miles to the house of a relative. She had formed a great resolution to save enough money to buy a Bible of her own. For years she had been hoarding up her chance pennies until when she was sixteen years old she found she had the price of a Bible in her hands.

Mary gets her Bible

She started out happily to walk the twenty-eight miles to the only place she knew where Bibles were sold. Her way lay along difficult and lonely paths through the mountains from Llanfihangel to Bala. When she reached Bala, tired and hungry, but happy in the accomplishment of her long-cherished purpose, she found that Mr. Charles, who was in charge of the depository, had sold the last copy he had. Strangely stirred by the child's tears and the revelation of her spiritual hunger, Mr. Charles gave her the only copy he had, one which had been laid aside on order of one of his friends. Fatigue and hunger were forgotten, as, tightly holding the Book in her hands, Mary Jones hastened to walk the long miles between her and home.

Why not for the world?

When Mr. Charles had finished his story with an appeal for the publication of a new edition of the Welsh Bible, Rev. Joseph Hughes, minister of the Baptist congregation at Battersea and Secretary of the Committee, said in words that have become historic, "Surely a society might be formed for the purpose. But if for Wales, why not for the kingdom? Why not for the world?"

The British and Foreign Bible Society organized

The proposition took fire. Week by week it was discussed in churches and newspapers. Mr. Hughes wrote an essay with the sort of ponderous title so dearly beloved in those days, "The Excellency of the Holy Scriptures; an Argument for their more general Dispersion." In this widely circulated pamphlet Mr. Hughes appealed to the public to assist in founding "the first institution that ever emanated from one nation for the good of all." Other meetings were held in the hospitable counting house of Mr. Joseph Hardcastle at Old Swan Stairs, in which the proposition was debated again and again, and a code of regulations gradually took shape which later became the constitution of the British and Foreign Bible Society. The name was the happy suggestion of Joseph Hughes.

Difficulties and obstacles

There were, of course, much opposition and many obstacles. Old General Conservatism, backed by his doughty lieutenants, Indifference and Sectarianism, did all he could to put down such an unprecedented enterprise. Added to the usual opposition which any new project must overcome, there were the formidable obstacles which the condition of the times presented. England was fighting for her life with Napoleon, who was confidently waiting for his 'six hours' mastery of the channel. Yet in such a time the Society was born.

Stormy times no bar to missions

Troublous times have no terrors for the missionary enterprise. Like a stormy petrel it rides the waves. When Europe was convulsed with the French Revolution, William Carey launched the modern enterprise of foreign missions. The first American societies were founded during the period of the war of 1812; the Women's Boards of Foreign Missions, during, and immediately after, the Civil War of 1861. During the last great war missionary societies have found a new response to their cause in many countries.

Charter of the British and Foreign Bible Society

The catholicity of the constitution of the British and Foreign Bible Society is the more remarkable in that it was made during a period of bitter sectarian conflicts between churchpersons and nonconformists. Christians of all communions united in its formation. The constitution then adopted is virtually that of the present day. The society was to limit its work to the printing and circulation of the Bible without note or comment. It was not to supplant, but to supplement, agencies already in the field, such as the Church Missionary Society, the Sunday School Union, the Religious Tract Society. The servant of all, it was to be the rival of none.

Rapid extension of the society

The expansion of the new society was rapid. Challenged by the violence and atheism set free during the throes of the French Revolution, the hearts of Christian men turned, even as they are turning today, with passionate eagerness to a fresh study of the Bible. Within twelve years the operations of the society had extended to Greenland and Canada, to Australia and the South Seas, to India and China and the Malay Archipelago, to the backwoods of America, the plantations of the West Indies, to Brazil and Chile. These foreign grants came at that very moment when the first faint tappings of the translators were heard from the other side of Christianity's world tunnel. Without the timely grants of the British and Foreign Bible Society the first Bibles of Carey and Marshman, of Morrison and Gützlaff and Moffat could with difficulty have been published.

The Welsh get their Bible

In the homeland the Welsh got their Bibles. Ten thousand copies of the New Testament were brought to Bala in 1806. When the people knew that the cart containing the books was on the road they went out to meet it and drew it into town with songs and rejoicings, as did the Israelites the ark. Every copy was eagerly bought. Late in the summer twilight young heads bent above the Book, by the glimmer of rushlight aged faces in many a little cottage pored over the precious pages, and laborers carried the Book to the fields with them in the early morning. Mary Jones's Bible, her name written on the fly leaf in her own handwriting, is one of the treasures of the British and Foreign Bible Society. Bibles were circulated by the thousand in the industrial towns like Bristol and Manchester and among the prisoners in the festering jails and prisons. From the first the policy of selling rather than giving Bibles was adopted.

Bible schools in the Scotch highlands

In the wild highlands of Scotland, a land then almost as little known as Tasmania, there lived 300,000 Highlanders who spoke no language but Gaelic. An edition of Gaelic Bibles was immediately put on the press for them, and in 1807 Gaelic Testaments were to be had for 10d. and whole Bibles for 3s. 6d. Many Highlanders walked great distances to obtain these books. Little Bible schools sprung up in the mountains, where old men learned to read in their own tongue the wonderful Word of God.

Bibles in five tongues in Great Britain

During the first twelve years of its history the British and Foreign Bible Society printed and distributed Bibles and Testaments to the number of 1,605,222 in the five languages of the British Isles; English, Gaelic, Erse, Manx, and Welsh. Auxiliaries sprang up in town and country; among them the Edinburgh Bible Society, the Dublin or Hibernian Bible Society, the Glasgow Bible Society, and societies many, big and little, in English cities and towns. The country was wretchedly poor, the national debt was crushing, the potato crop had failed, but the people pressed forward to buy Bibles. "We'll buy a little less meal and take home the Word of God with us," they said. A poor blind beggar with five children bought a Testament. "I would grieve less to know that my child was hungry," she said, "than to have it live without the Word of God."

Expansion on the continent

From Great Britain the society promptly extended its work to the continent of Europe in a very Pentecost of interest in the Bible. An Icelandic Bible was brought out and an auxiliary founded in Iceland. A Bible society was organized in Stockholm, which later became the National Bible Society of Sweden. Societies were established in Denmark, Germany, France, the Netherlands, Austria, and Switzerland. In 1813 the St. Petersburg Bible Society was founded in the presence of members of state and nobles and the highest dignitaries of the church. In every case these societies were helped to organize by grants from the treasury of the British and Foreign Bible Society.

The Russian Bible Society

Later some of these societies incurred the hostility of the hierarchy and were suppressed. The Russian Bible Society was under the protection of the Czar, who had ordered the New Testament introduced into schools and colleges. The people in many villages gathered to listen to the words of the Savior. Bibles were reaching the prisoners and the sailors. Then the Holy Synod took fright. They feared the effect of the Bible on the common people and in 1826 were strong enough to bring about the edict suppressing the Russian Bible Society, which at that time had two hundred and eighty-nine auxiliaries.

Fortunes of continental Bible societies

The Pope, too, took action against the circulation of the Scriptures in Poland and Austria, and reactionary governments often made its circulation difficult. Some of these continental societies organized in the early decades of the nineteenth century have persisted. Fifty were listed at the time of the Edinburgh Conference in 1910. For the most part, however, these societies have confined their work to the publication of Bibles in their own language, leaving the greater part of the publication of Bibles for the non-Christian lands to the three great societies of the English-speaking world.

The Scotch Bible Society

The National Bible Society of Scotland grew directly out of the Edinburgh Auxiliary of the British and Foreign Bible Society. The separation came when a difference of view arose in regard to the including of the apocryphal Books in the Bible. To this the Scotch objected, and, although a concession was made to their views, it did not come in time to avoid the foundation of a separate society.

Beginnings of Bible society in America

The first Bible society in America was organized in Philadelphia in 1808. This was aided by the British and Foreign Bible Society, by a grant of one thousand dollars and a supply of the Scriptures in Welsh, Gaelic, French, and German for use among the immigrant peoples of those days. The following year six more Bible societies were formed, among them the New York and Massachusetts societies. As soon as these societies were formed and a systematic inquiry made in regard to the supply of Bibles, it was found that many communities had hardly a Bible. In 1812, when Louisiana was admitted to the Union, a long search was made for a Bible on which to administer the oath of office. At last a priest was discovered who had a copy of the Latin Vulgate. It was estimated that there were at least 78,000 families destitute of the Word of God.

Organization of American Bible Society

In 1816 a convention of delegates representing thirty-one institutions was called in New York City, and the American Bible Society was organized. Some of the most distinguished men of the nation were present at the meeting. Among them was Hon. Elias Boudinot, then president of the New Jersey

Bible Society, and distinguished for his services during the revolution; Samuel J. Mills, a moving spirit in the first organized foreign mission work in America; Rev. Lyman Beecher, John Griscom, Valentine Mott, the great surgeon; Joseph C. Hornblower, later Chief Justice of New Jersey; James Fenimore Cooper, Eliphalet Nott, William Jay, Col. Richard Varick, and others hardly less distinguished. The following week, May 13, 1816, a great ratification meeting was held in the Sessions Court Room of New York's beautiful new City Hall, now the Board of Estimates room in New York's beautiful old City Hall.

Distinguished names in the society

The first president of the society was Boudinot; and Hon. John Jay, the first chief justice of the United States, became first vice president and later the second president of the society. From that day to the present a long line of distinguished Americans have backed the Society with their influence and their active support. President John Quincy Adams for thirty years continued his active connection with the society Other Presidents, Andrew Jackson, Zachary Taylor, Ulysses S. Grant, Rutherford B. Hayes, Benjamin Harrison, Grover Cleveland, Theodore Roosevelt, and Woodrow Wilson have, by their outspoken advocacy, furthered the great ends of the society. So have Chief Justices Marshall, Chase, and Fuller, and Justices McLean, Harlan, Brewer, Hughes, and other members of the Supreme Court. Many governors have given their hearty support, among them DeWitt Clinton, who while governor of New York came down from Albany regularly to attend the monthly meetings of the board of managers. If one were to run over the names of the men who have made the America of the last one hundred years, it is safe to say that the great majority of them have been men who honestly and cordially recognized the supreme value of the Bible in our national civilization, and were true friends of the American Bible Society.

Bible recognized by founders of the Republic

The founders of the Republic realized the importance of the Bible, before any Bible society had been organized in the whole world. Once in 1777 and again in 1782 the Congress of the United States took official action toward the obtaining and supplying of Bibles. England had retained the publication of the Bible in her own hands. None were published in the colonies, and so with the opening of the revolution the supply of Bibles was cut off. In 1777 Congress authorized its committee to import 20,000 copies of the Bible. "This order was accordingly made." In 1782 the first English Bible ever printed in the United States, that printed by Robert Aitken of Philadelphia, was put out under the auspices of Congress by the passage of the following resolution:

> Sept. 2, 1782
>
> RESOLVED, that the United States in Congress assembled . . . recommend this edition of the Bible to the inhabitants of the United States.
>
> (Signed) Charles Thomson,
> Secretary

Common characteristics of the great Bible societies

Such in brief is the story of the characteristics of the great founding of the three great Bible Societies of the English-speaking nations. Certain principles and policies characterize all three.

1. *The printing of the Scripture without note or comment.* This wise restriction has made it possible to serve churches of the most divergent views.
2. Publishing of translations into the languages of the non-Christian world.
3. Selling the books at so low a price as to put them within the reach of the poorest. In pursuance of this policy Bibles are often sold at a mere fraction of their cost.
4. The printing of separate portions as well as entire Testaments and Bibles.
5. Defraying the cost of translations in the various mission fields of the world.

In pursuance of their policy of translating the Scriptures these and the European Bible societies have pushed out to the rim of the world, until today the Bible is the universal Book. The prime reason for requiring the immigrants at Ellis Island to demonstrate their ability to read by reading from the Testament is because it is the only book published in all the languages spoken by the immigrants.

Value of Bible societies in missionary enterprise

Without the cooperation of these great Bible societies it is difficult to see how the preparation of the translations could have been financed. Year after year grants have been made to some missionary or committee in aid of the translation of the Bible. The first book ever published by the British and Foreign Bible Society in 1809, was St. John's Gospel in the language of the Mohawk Indians, a great expense for few people. The same society voted Morrison $50,000 for expenses incurred in preparing and printing his first Chinese Bible. With no niggardly hand the societies cooperate with the missionaries, preparing the versions, printing the editions, and sending them out, carriage free, to stations often most remote. From one agency in one year missions of seventeen different denominations have been supplied with Bibles.

Enormous and continuous sale of the Bible

The enormous and continuous sale of the Bible staggers belief. Year after year, decade after decade, the sale goes on, gathering volume as it goes. It is difficult to bring together the total sales. There are the Bible societies, the commercial publishing houses such as the Oxford Press, or the Nelsons; there are denominational publishing houses; missions such as the Scripture Gift Mission, the Pocket Testament League, the Los Angeles Bible House, and scores of others. It is estimated that 35 million Bibles, Testaments, and Gospels were issued in 1919, three-fourths of which were published by the Bible societies throughout the world. In 1913 Japan bought 586,667 Bibles, Testaments, and Gospels. For several years the Bible has been the best-seller in Japan, as it has in China, which in 1916 bought 2,271,771 copies of either Bible, Testament, or Gospel; in 1913 Korea purchased 389,401. The Filipino people in 1917 bought 119,409 volumes in fifteen languages.

Sales of Bible compared with those of other books

The significance of the sale of the Bible is seen only when its sales are compared with those of other books. In Christian countries there is no novelty to commend it, yet it sells steadily without any press agents or book notices. The most popular modern English author is Charles Dickens. It has been computed that since *Pickwick Papers* appeared 25 million copies of Dickens' works have been published. The Bible sold 35 million in one year. Said a New York book-seller, "You may talk as you will of your multitudinous editions of popular novels, but the Bible leads them all, year in and year out." It is difficult to realize how many 35 million books are. Suppose, beginning at New York City and traveling to San Francisco, eight Bibles or Testaments were deposited at the foot of each telegraph pole beside the railroad track, there would be forty thousand left, out of the first million, when the Golden

Gate of San Francisco was reached. At the end of the thirty-sixth crossing of the continent, after consuming at least three months of time, there would be 440,000 Bibles remaining undeposited.

Christ's vagabonds The Bible societies do more than finance Bible translation and print all kinds of editions of the Bible, big and little, and sell innumerable copies. They promote its sales through peddlers of the Book, Bible Vagabonds, Christ's Wanderers. No chapter of Christian heroism is more splendid than that which recounts the story of the colporter, humble like his master, and like his Master going about to do good. The colporter is ubiquitous. You can not lose him. If you ascend to the frozen North, he is there; if you bury yourself in the steamy depths of a South American river forest, he is ahead of you; if you climb the Himalayas and penetrate some high pass in Tibet, you will find his footprints. On his bicycle he hums along the highways of the Far West; on his snowshoes he finds the lumberjacks in the big timber; his trusty Ford is seen skimming over the plains He paddles down still rivers in an African dugout, or packs his Bibles on a Russian sled in the frozen fastnesses of Siberia.

Colporters in every land These colporters are of all races as well as in every nation. They are the John the Baptists who prepare in the desert a highway for the missionaries.

It was a Japanese colporter who was visiting the schools in Kagoshima in January 1914, and trying to sell Bibles to the students in a large medical school:

> "I don't want to read any ancient conceptions of two thousand years ago," said a student scornfully.
>
> "The sun was created millions of years ago," said the colporter, "but its light still warms us." And he sold his book.

It was a Chinese colporter who reported, "When I come to villages where I have often been before, the children run to meet me, crying, 'The man with the heavenly books is here.' "

It was another Chinese colporter, Khoo Chiang Bee of Singapore, who took long journeys to Sumatra and Johore, which necessitated his leaving wife and family for months, while he carried the Bible to hostile Moslem villages and actually succeeded in selling 12,800 copies of the Scriptures.

It was a Bulgarian colporter who came upon a gipsy camp and read the Gospel to them until midnight, with the result that they bought all his store of Testaments and Psalters.

It was a Belgian colporter, Canfriez, who got up every morning at 4:30 for nine days in succession that he might sell his Bibles during the popular pilgrimages near Namur.

It was a Manchurian colporter who preached daily and sold Bibles at the Mongolian Temple Fair where 2,300 Buddhist lamas were assembled.

It was a Tamil colporter in South India who gave Gospels to some palm-climbers in exchange for cocoanuts, because they had no money.

It was Old Kim, the tiger hunter, whom Bishop Lambuth met in Korea, "a grizzled old man with weather-beaten face and sunburned neck and shoulders furrowed by the claws of more than one tiger. 'What have you in that bag, Brother Kim?'

'Ammunition' was his laconic reply with a smile, as he showed his New Testament and hymn book. 'Do you no longer hunt tigers?'

'No, Moksa, I am hunting for men.' "

Colporters of true heroic stuff

It was a Chinese colporter who sold himself as a slave so that in the hold of a coolie ship on the voyage to South America and in the mines he might tell his countrymen of Jesus.

They were Tahitian sellers of the Book whose canoe was overturned one day in the boiling surf two miles off shore. When William Ellis went to their rescue he found the men supporting themselves on their paddles. They said that when the canoe sunk they forgot to be afraid of the sharks because they were thinking about their Bibles carefully wrapped in cloth and tied to the mast.

It was English George Borrow, most noted of colporters, who edited the Manchu New Testament in St. Petersburg, took journeys that carried him to the remotest parts of Spain, and out of them wrote his famous and altogether delightful *Bible in Spain*.

It was a Greek colporter who visited every house in Athens in 1913.

New Testament in Japanese prisons

In Japan, through the cooperation of the missionaries and the churches, a copy of the New Testament has been given recently to each of the twenty-six thousand prisoners in the part of Japan served by the American Bible Society. The great undertaking was conceived in the heart of a humble Japanese colporter who went out to walk one Sunday morning and passed by the big prison in Kofu. As he thought of the wretched prisoners within the gloomy pile, he remembered his own salvation from a life of sin by Christ; his heart melted in compassion, and a voice seemed to say, "Tomorrow go there with your Bibles." He secured permission of the prison officials to present each of the eight hundred prisoners with a New Testament, if the books could be given free of charge. Confident that the Lord would supply him the funds, he stepped into the store of a prosperous merchant—not a Christian—and told him his story. "That is just what I would be glad to do! I will give you the money," said the merchant.

A prison officer impressed

Within a week several carloads of New Testaments were at the prison gate and the surprised official, who had never expected that his conditions could be fulfilled, was saying, "Why is it that you have worked with such energy, baffled by no obstacles, to do this thing for these miserable men? I cannot understand it."

For over an hour the colporter opened the Scriptures and preached unto him Jesus. With tears in his eyes the official said, "Thank you for what you have done and said. I have known little about Christianity, but now for the first time I have some understanding of the true spirit of your Christ."

Gifts from Japanese Christians

The changed attitude of the Japanese government is seen in the fact that permission was given later to carry out the larger project of giving a Testament to the twenty-six thousand prisoners. When the project was known money began to come in from the missionaries, the churches, and the Sunday schools. Baron Morimura heard of it and sent three hundred yen. He was himself converted by reading Kochi Sari's book, *My Twenty-three Years in Prison*, and ever since his conversion has been deeply interested in work among prisoners.

Since this distribution of Bibles the Christian governor of Kosuge prison reports that the government has made it a rule to furnish each new prisoner's cell with a copy of both the Christian and the Buddhist Scriptures.

Chirst in a Korean prison

It is only necessary to allude to the story of Syngman Rhee, the highly educated young Korean revolutionist, who was converted by reading the New Testament while suffering the agonies of one of the fetid prisons of the old days in Korea. In the prison with his feet in the stocks he cried, "O God, save my country, save my soul!" When he found Christ, he began to witness to the prisoners and to the jailer who, like that jailer long ago, believed with all his house and was baptized.

Dr. Rhee conducted classes for the prisoners and before his release had won more than forty to Christ, men perfected in suffering, who went forth for the regeneration of Korea. Dr. Rhee himself left Korea when Japan took control, and went to the Hawaiian Islands, where he was appointed director of schools for the very large Korean population by the Hawaiian Conference of the Methodist Episcopal church. Sherwood Eddy tells his story fully in his book, *The New Era in Asia*.

A Chinese philanthropist gives New Testament

It was the Bible that found Mr. Yung Tao, a rich and successful business man of Peking, who since 1900 has devoted himself to philanthropy and social welfare. So interested was he in the development of his nation that he undertook the education of four hundred young men in the Y.M.C.A. schools in North China. After a long search through the various religions of the world he applied himself to the study of the Bible and became convinced of its supreme value. In 1914 he bought five thousand New Testaments, some of them in expensive bindings, to present to his friends. In 1915 he gave an order for ten thousand Chinese Bibles in special binding, saying that it was his intention ultimately to distribute fifty thousand. Each of these Bibles contained a slip saying, "Respectfully presented by Yung Tao, who is not a church member." Not contented with giving Bibles, recommending them, and joining the Centenary Committee of the American Bible Society, Yung Tao gave an hour every day to the further study of the Bible with Mr. Edwards of the Peking Y.M.C.A. The result was that he who had so steadfastly commended the Book while declaring that he was not himself a Christian became a humble, ardent disciple of Jesus, and was baptized by Rev. Chauncey Goodrich at the time of the Bible Society Centenary, May 17, 1916. Twenty-seven others were baptized with him. That afternoon in Central Park, a beautiful place filled with huge old cypress trees, Yung Tao spoke before four thousand people of the power of the Bible to change men's hearts.

The Bible finds a Hindu fakir

A Hindu *fakir* with matted hair and ash-besmeared body was sitting lost in meditation, when he chanced to see some torn leaves of a book, a part of John's Gospel, which someone had tossed away. He read words that were like water to one dying of thirst. He showed his torn leaves to an Englishman and asked him if he obeyed it. The Englishman confessed his faith in it, and as he handed it back the *fakir* noticed that he wore black band on his sleeve. Concluding that this was the caste mark of one who obeyed the wonderful *shastra* he had found, the *fakir* put a black band on his own arm, as the badge of his new faith. Months later he wandered into a Christian church and pointed to his arm-band as proof of his discipleship. When he learned that it was an English sign of the death of some loved one, he said, "But I read in the Book that my Loved One has died, so I shall wear it in memory of him." When later he received an entire New Testament and learned the gospel of the resurrection, a new light shone in his face; and this became the badge of his discipleship instead of the black band which he took from his arm.

Ministry to the soldiers

In addition to the regular work of the Bible societies there is their wonderful ministry to the soldiers in time of war. In the Crimean and Franco-Prussian Wars, the War of Italian Liberation, the Boer War, the Russo-Japanese War, and, most of all, in the great World War the presses have been kept running night and day to supply the demands of the army. The American Bible Society has issued for the use of soldiers and sailors, since the World War began, 4,541,455 volumes. For the fighting forces in Europe the society has supplied 1,846,488 Scriptures in whole or in part since the War began. The British and Foreign Bible Society has distributed 7 million Bibles, Testaments, and portions during the same period, not only among the troops of the British Empire, and the Allies and assistants, but also among all their foes, in the very ranks of their bitterest enemies. The National Bible Society of Scotland has distributed during four and one-half years 5,020,000 Bibles, Testaments, or portions. In all more than 16.5 million copies have been distributed in eighty-one languages; thirty-four languages originating in Europe, five in Asia Minor, twelve in Asia, eighteen in Africa, three in North America, and nine in the Islands of the Seas.

Such a distribution, with the accompanying firsthand acquaintance of the Scriptures gained by soldiers not alone in the camps and hospitals of Europe, but in Egypt, in war-torn equatorial Africa, in Arabia, Mesopotamia, Syria, Asia Minor, Persia, and China, is one of the profoundest efforts for the furtherance of the gospel proceeding from the great World War. A sower has indeed gone forth to sow on the blood-stained fields of war. Some of the harvests will wave with golden grain a century hence.

Widespread contributions to the fund

The great distribution enlisted widespread interest. The New York Globe conducted a campaign yielding $5,000,

The Atlanta Journal $4,490, and from thirty-two other daily newspapers from every part of the country came equally energetic and enthusiastic support. "Governors, members of Congress, judges, philanthropists, editors, merchants, mechanics, clerks, sisters, mothers, housemaids, children, G.A.R. veterans, officers and soldiers in the ranks, churches, banks, department stores, theatres" all helped. The money came in large gifts, small gifts, gifts of jewelry, of Liberty Bonds, of precious mementoes. Gifts came, too, from the ends of the earth. General Hsiung Keh-Wu, commander-in-chief of the southern forces in Szechuan, sent two hundred Bank of China notes ($80.00) saying, "I know that what the Bible teaches makes men and nations great."

Approval of military leaders

The distribution of Bibles among the troops had the warm approval of the great military leaders. The commander-in-chief of the Allied armies, General Foch, wrote to the New York Bible Society:

> La Bible est certainement le meilleur viatique que vous puissiez donner au Soldat Americain partant a la Bataille pour entretenir son magnifique ideal et sa foi.

Pershing cabled, "I am glad to see that every man in the army is to have a Testament. Its teachings will fortify us for our great task." Leonard Wood wrote, "If we can put the spirit of the Bible into our army, we need have no fear of the result." Field Marshal Haig sent a message to the American soldier through the New York Bible Society, "Knock impossibilities on the head; do it now. God is with you." Field Marshal Lord Roberts said to the British troops when crossing the channel, "You will find in this little volume guidance when you are in health, comfort when you are in sickness, and strength when you are in adversity." Vice President Thomas R. Marshall wrote, "The pocket New Testament is the most valuable thing which the soldier carries into the fight with him." President Wilson wrote, "They (the men of the army and navy) will need the support of the only Book from which they can get it." Theodore Roosevelt wrote to the American Bible Society, "Every soldier and sailor of the United States should have a Testament." Abraham Lincoln said it all long ago, during the years of the Civil War, when he said of the Bible, "It is the best Book that God has given to men."

The boys welcome the Testament

That the Testaments were joyfully received no one could doubt who ever saw the boys standing in line to get them, or read their letters which poured into the Bible House in a steady stream.

"I've been reading this and it has changed my life," Fighting Pat O'Brien of the Royal Flying Corps wrote. "A lot of men who have never thought much about religion are thinking about it now. I believe they will read those little khaki Testaments and I am sure they will get help from them."

"It is strange how some people are affected by things," remarked the camp secretary. "Now there was that private at Camp Custer. He wanted a Testament, although he could neither read nor write. 'I can't read,' he said, 'but I like to feel one in my pocket.'"

The Pocket Testament League

More than seventy thousand men signed the cards, "I accept Christ," in the handsome little Pocket-League Testament. These Testaments were presented personally to the men in the camps by members of the Business Men's War Council of the Pocket Testament League, who toured the camps giving out great numbers of them to those who would join the Pocket Testament League by promising to carry a Testament with them always, and to make a practice of reading it daily.

Story of its beginnings

The story of the Pocket Testament League itself is a wonderful example of the living power of the gospel. Some years ago Miss Cadbury, a young girl living in Birmingham, England, decided always to carry a Testament in her pocket. Other girls did the same. Later the league was extended to all sorts and conditions of men and women. In 1908, when Miss Cadbury became Mrs. Charles M. Alexander, her husband and Dr. J. Wilbur Chapman launched the league to endeavor to get people to read at least a chapter a day. More than 365,000 British soldiers joined the league during the four years of the war.

In the valley of the shadow

In this war, as in every other since the British and Foreign Bible Society began its ministry, one hundred years ago, out of the depths men have cried unto God. After the bloody battle of Stone River during the Civil War, a lad of nineteen was found dead, leaning against the stump of a tree. His dead eyes were open, his face smiling, his hand laid on his open Bible at the words, "Yea, though I walk through the valley of the shadow of death, I will fear no evil; for thou art with me."

Seed sown by the wayside

Thousands have taken the books and got no good; thousands have carried them in their pockets as a talisman and felt little benefit; some have thrown them away or sold them; but thousands upon thousands have discovered the Word of God, and in that discovery have found their Father. Such a sowing in the blood-drenched fields of war has never been known.

Some practical pointers for Bible lovers

Pointing morals is not fashionable, but there are some morals that point like a gyroscopic compass. The facts of this chapter certainly have practical bearings on every Christian life:

1. The duty and privilege of joining the army of Bible readers.
2. The financial support of the Bible societies.
3. The custom of carrying about Testaments or Bible portions in the language of some immigrant peoples and giving them out as opportunity offers.
4. The launching of a national campaign of Bible selling and Bible distribution.
5. Increased honor of the Bible in our churches and homes.
6. Furthering the enrollment in the Pocket Testament League.
7. A campaign of newspaper publicity.

Financial support of the societies

It is to be feared that thousands of individuals and churches do not realize that the great Bible societies need continuous financial support if they are to maintain their blessed ministry. In the early years Bible Day was regularly observed each year in hundreds of churches. Now in thousands it is never mentioned. If every Sunday School member were asked to give five cents annually on a Bible Day, in which the glorious ministry of the American Bible Society was clearly presented, a fund of a million dollars a year would be placed in the hands of the society. What this would mean in extending the influence of the Word of God, no words are vigorous enough to express. Some denominations have a noble record of faithful support of the Bible society. Others are not so well represented. Doubtless this is through failure to recognize that funds are actually needed. A perusal of the annual report of the American Bible Society will reveal whether our own church is honoring its devotion to the Bible in this tangible evidence of interest.

Outline

Chapter 5

AIM: To show that the Bible has a message for nations; that nations are held accountable for national sins; that the Bible conceptions lie at the bottom of all that is best in the laws and ideals of modern Christian nations, and that in the non-Christian nations the influence of the Bible is plainly seen.

I. The Bible Message for Nations
   1. Their accountability to the laws of God
   2. Their punishment for national sins

II. Biblical Foundations in Modern Christian Nations
   1. Influence on the arts
   2. Influence on law
      a. European codes
      b. Roman law
      c. English law (Illustrations)
      d. American laws (Testimony of great people)
   3. Influence through continuous education of church festivals and ordinances
      a. The Sabbath, Sunday schools, Christmas, Easter
      b. Baptism, the Lord's Supper

III. The Bible's Influence on Non-Christian Lands

1. India, seen in growing appreciation of thoughtful men, changing status of women, loosening of caste bonds, rise of the Christian community
2. Africa, Uganda, among the Sechuana, the Hottentots
3. New Zealand among the Maori
4. Pacific Islands, testimony of Darwin; service and testimony of Chalmers and Paton
5. Korea, a nation of people of the Book
6. Japan, influence of early Christians, testimony of Count Okuma, changing status of women, prison reform, functioning of Christian conscience.
7. China, influence of Christian missionaries, diplomats, education. Testimony of great officials.

IV. The Bible Goes Back to Its Homeland

Five

The Bible's Influence on Civilization

> "Hold fast to the Bible as the sheet-anchor to your liberties; write its precepts in your hearts, and practice them in your lives. To the influence of this Book we are indebted for all progress made in our true civilization, and to this we must look as our guide in the future."
>
> *U.S. Grant, 18th president of the U.S.*

Topic of chapter In preceding chapters we have outlined the Bible's own missionary character and message, have shown the enormous enterprise accomplished by Bible translators in furthering the worldwide propagation of the Christian message, and have discussed the rise and activities of the great Bible societies which have made possible the worldwide distribution of the Scripture, through the cooperation of the various missionary agencies. In the present chapter we are to study the influence which the Bible exerts not alone upon individuals, but upon nations.

The Bible has message to nations The Bible has a message to the nations. It contains the story of one nation chosen by God for a great mission to the whole world. It addresses the nations almost as superpersonalities, and plainly recognizes them as having an organic life and a national responsibility to the God of nations. Human society according to the Bible rests on no "social contract," but inheres in the plan of the Creator, who made humankind and nations to be members of one another in one great human family.

National sins pay national penalities

So strong is the sense of responsibility to God on the part of nations and of smaller social groups that the Bible is full of reproofs and dooms pronounced against those nations which forsook God. Jesus' woe pronounced upon Capernaum and Bethsaida (Matt 11:20-25) is in line with the dooms which the prophets pronounced against nations and cities at the very hour when their arrogant wickedness strutted defiant before the face of God. These prophecies make great reading to the traveler in Mesopotamia and Syria. A colonel in the Turkish army once asked Dr. Cyrus Hamlin in Constantinople for a proof that the Bible is the word of God. Dr. Hamlin did not immediately answer, but, learning that the colonel was a traveled man, he said to him:

"Have you ever been in Babylon?"

"Yes," replied the colonel, "and I will tell you a curious incident. The ruins of Babylon abound in game; and once, engaging a sheikh with his followers, I arrived among the ruins for a week's shooting. At sundown the Arabs, to my amazement, began to strike their tents. I went to the sheikh and protested most strongly. I was paying him handsomely, but I now offered to double the amount; but nothing I could say had any effect.

'It is not safe,' said the sheikh, 'no mortal flesh dare stay here after sunset. Ghosts and ghouls come out of the holes and caverns after dark, and whomsoever they capture becomes one of themselves. No Arab has ever seen the sun go down on Babylon.'"

Dr. Hamlin took out his Bible and read from the thirteenth of Isaiah: "And Babylon, the glory of kingdoms, the beauty of the Chaldeans' pride, shall be as when God overthrew Sodom and Gomorrah. It shall never be inhabited, neither shall it be dwelt in from generation to generation; neither shall the Arabian pitch tent there, . . . but wild beasts of the desert shall lie there, . . . and wolves shall cry in their castles, and jackals in the pleasant palaces" (Isaiah 13:19).

"That is history you have been reading," said the Turk.

"No," said Dr., Hamlin, "it is prophecy. Those words were written when Babylon was in all her glory; and you know what Babylon is today"

Biblical foundations of modern civilizaton

No teaching is more needed today than the plain Bible doctrine that God has a will for the nations; that they are subject to his law, that those who break it will be punished as nations; that the kingdom of God is no iridescent dream, but a great reality to be accomplished in this world through our cooperation with the God of nations in the upbuilding of human society. Were there opportunity in this brief sketch, it would be of wonderful interest to study the way in which the Bible has been wrought into the very substance of our civilization, modifying, or creating many of its features. Imperfectly obeyed and only partially known as the Bible teachings have been, they have laid the foundations of all that is glorious in modern civilization. There is room barely to allude to this phase of the question, since our main business is with the influence of the Bible in the nations among which the modern missionary enterprise is at work.

The Bible influences the arts

The change from the roll to the parchment volume was made by the church in the copying of the Bible, so that we are indebted to the Bible that we read from "*biblia*" and not from rolls. In the illuminating of the old vellum manuscripts of the Bible, in the decorating of the churches with paintings of scriptural scenes, in the manufacture of jeweled cups and chalices, in the weaving of altar cloths, the artisans of the middle ages found the inspiration of their crafts. Lamps, cups of glass or gold or silver, ivory tablets and carvings, vestments and curtains, cathedrals and town halls, all show the ever-present influence of the Bible. The architects, the painters, the sculptors, the gold, and silversmiths, the leather workers, the carpenters, the weavers, the lace-workers, all found the Bible molding and developing their crafts. Says Von Dobschütz:

> It was the Christian church which served to keep the old civilization alive through all troubles and dangers. When classical training had nearly vanished everywhere else, it was found in some remote monasteries. Esteem of good style, love of ancient poetry, some chance bits of philosophy had safely weathered the storm. But it was only in combination with the Bible that those remains of classical reading were allowed to persist. The mediaeval civilization was Biblical at its base.

The Bible influences law

A young man who thought himself an unbeliever started to read law. As he read Blackstone's *Commentaries* he continually came upon references to the laws of Moses as a source undoubted and indisputable. Turning to study the Bible, which he had always neglected and despised, he was surprised to find how its principles underlay law, and, as he read, he became himself a believer. When King

Alfred the Great collected together the old Saxon laws for his people, he put the Ten Commandments at the beginning as the basal law of the land. The old German collections likewise, *Schwabenspiegel, Sachsenspiegel*, etc., present the law as based on the law of God contained in the Bible. The Canon Law quite naturally incorporated much from the Bible, though it often departed widely from its spirit in favor of more autocratic sources. The wonderful body of human law was also deeply affected by principles derived from the Bible. The principles underlying Hebrew laws and the teachings of the New Testament were so wrought into the structure of Roman law in the codes of Theodosius and Justinian as permanently to shape it. (See Millman's *Latin Christianity,* vol. 1, chap. 5.)

The Bible in English law

English law was least influenced by Roman law. "Down through the ages," says Tenney in his *Contrasts in Social Progress,* "they (the English) pushed phrase upon phrase of Christian edict. . . . He will never understand how justice has come into the English world and fair dealing and kindness between neighbors, purity and self-control, who does not detect the hoary heads of sermons upon the pages of its black-letter law books. In the reign of Henry VIII one hundred and sixty chancellors, and all the masters of the rolls during the first twenty-six years, were clergymen. The moral principles of Christianity as elaborated during many centuries were thus transmuted daily into law." Take for example the statement of Edward the Confessor: "We know that through God's grace a thrall has become a thane, and a churl has become an earl, a singer a priest, and a scribe a bishop; and formerly, as God decreed, a fisher became a bishop. We have all one heavenly Father, one spiritual mother which is called the Church, and we are therefore brothers."

"Christian law, the guardian angel of a hundred generations, the absolute justice of the state, enlightened by the perfect reason of the state, is little else than the attempt to reduce the golden rule to practice," says Choate.

"In two minutes I can tell you how to be a good lawyer—as good a lawyer as anybody," said Governor Briggs of Massachusetts. "Just look over your case carefully, understand it, and then do what you think is right, and in nine cases out of ten you will have the law on your side."

Slow conquest of biblical ideals

Great evils, to be sure, have been trenched in the law of Christian lands for centuries. The principles of the Bible have penetrated slowly and with infinite difficulty into the violent and cruel lives of men; but, when once it has been clearly seen by any great number of the people that a cause, an institution, or a form of government is contrary to the Gospel, that day the cause, or institution, or government is doomed.

The Bible influences the Constitution of United States

When we turn to our own country for an illustration of the influence of the Bible on national life and customs and character, the evidence is overwhelming. The pilgrim fathers came to America that they might freely carry out the principles they found in their Bibles. A small band of them protested against current ideas of political and religious freedom and were driven into the wilderness of Rhode Island. There they planted a state based squarely upon the principles of soul liberty, individual accountability, and God's government of nations. Ultimately they have given their ideals to the whole nation, as Oscar Strauss points out in his *Life of Roger Williams.*

Illustrations of Bible's influence

(1) When Jefferson drew up the Declaration of Independence he stated that he had drawn many of the principles from his observations of the practices of self-government in a local Baptist church. The earlier Mecklenburg Declaration was drawn up by delegates of Presbyterian churches.

(2) It was Abraham Lincoln, a man steeped in the knowledge and love of the Bible, who blackened out from our laws the statutes permitting slavery.

(3) It was the Supreme Court of the United States which handed down a decision affirming that this is a Christian country.

Testimony of great men

There is an embarrassment of riches when one turns to the great men of all nations for their testimony regarding the influence of the Bible on civil law and the institutions of free government. Said John Quincy Adams, "In whatsoever light we regard the Bible, whether with reference to revelation, to history, or to morality, it is an invaluable and inexhaustible mine of knowledge and virtue." Wrote Horace Greeley, "It is impossible mentally or socially to enslave a Bible reading people. The principles of the Bible are the groundwork of human freedom." Queen Victoria gave a Bible to a pagan ambassador who had inquired the secret of England's greatness, saying, "This is the secret of England's greatness." Froude, in his essay on Calvinism, says, "All that we call modern civilization, in a sense which deserves the name, is the visible expression of the transforming power of the gospel." The new commissioner from the

Philippines, Teodora Yanco, said recently that his predecessor, Mr. Quezon, told him, "Study the Bible because the Bible is the underlying secret of American philanthropy. The business men of America have been launched into all kinds of philanthropic effort in behalf of their fellow men, because America is a land where the Bible is honored and read." Of the Bible said Garibaldi, "This is the cannon [*sic*] that will make Italy free." Six years ago the governor of Michigan declared in a message to the state legislature, "The Bible is our constitution of Christian civilization." Said Gladstone, "My only hope for the world is in bringing the human mind into contact with Divine revelation." Said G. Stanley Hall in an address on the teaching of morals, "To cultivate morality one must appeal, as the Bible does, to the moral sense rather than to reason. Hence life must be leavened with religion and children infected with Christianity." Of Justice Harlan of the Supreme Court it was said that he went to his rest each night with one hand on the Bible and the other on the Constitution of the United States.

The Bible influences music

Modern music was born in the service of the church. The greatest music that has ever been written is Christian in its occasion, theme, or inspiration. Outside of nations under the fructifying and radiant impulses of the gospel, no great music has ever arisen. The great masters have been the servants of the Bible.

The Bible influences through church ordinances and festivals

President Schurman of Cornell has commented on the educative power of the Christian Sabbath on our national life. Week after week, month after month, year after year, century after century, the hearts of the people are summoned to the thought of God through the recurring Christian festival of the Sabbath. At least 400,000 sermons based on the Bible are preached every week in gatherings held for religious purposes. We complain sometimes that people do not go to church. The miracle is that there is one topic which for fifty-two weeks in a year, for one hundred years in a century, can draw people out to hear it discussed by others of usually no more than ordinary ability. A great speaker might fill the largest hall on a political topic for two or three or possibly ten weeks running. There is no topic but religion which could get him an audience for a year, much less for two or ten. "Every period of English-speaking history assures us that our moral power increases or weakens with the rise or fall of Sabbath reverence," says McAfee in *The Greatest English Classic.* It is worthy of remark that no religion except the

Christian has developed anything comparable to the local congregational groups meeting weekly for social worship, fellowship, and instruction. This is a characteristic functioning of Christianity of enormous social power. Join to the Sabbath, the Sunday school, the Christmas and Easter festivals, the ordinances of baptism and the Lord's Supper, and you have a group of institutions whose steady pressure upon the national life is as immeasurable as it is unnoted.

The Bible influence on non-Christian nations Turning from Christian nations, or more properly nations on the road to become Christian, let us consider the marvelous transforming influence of the Bible as seen today at work in the so-called non-Christian nations of the world. In considering this we shall not emphasize the direct religious influence which is primarily exerted upon individuals, the cell-life of nations, but consider rather those lower and more obvious effects to be seen in customs and institutions. In reality when we know the revolutionary power of the Christian gospel upon individuals, we need not stop to consider anything else, since what changes the cell changes the organism. But in deference to our slowness-of-heart-to-believe in that which is spiritual and unseen the lesser inquiry has its place.

Influence of Bible on India India, one of the great heathen nations (non-Christian seems too weak a term to describe India's spiritual wire entanglements) has been longest under the impact of civilization colored by biblical conceptions and principles. India is one of the most difficult, if not the most difficult field in the world. Yet the traces of the Bible's influence in Indian life are written large for the one who runs to read. An address was delivered to the students in St. Paul's College, Calcutta, recently, by a leading Hindu, Sir Narayan Chandavarkar, which shows the estimate placed on the Bible by leaders of Indian thought, even though they do not avow themselves Christian. He showed the students his well-worn pocket New Testament, told them that it had been his daily companion for thirty years, and recommended to them his daily habit of reading the epistle of James before dawn, to lift their thoughts to God.

Said one of the Indian Rajahs, "If I were a missionary I would not argue, I would distribute the New Testament." If the royal gentleman had considered that even after a century of promotion of education by a Christian government and by Christian missions only one man in ten and one woman in a hundred can read, he might have recognized some other forms of Christian service as also needful.

It was the Maha-Rajah of Travancore who gave this testimony to the power of the Bible, "Where do the English get their knowledge, intelligence, cleverness, and power? It is their Bible which gives it to them; and now they have translated it into our language, bring it to us and say, 'Take it, read it, examine it, and see if it is not good.' Of one thing I am convinced, do what we will, oppose it as we may, it is the Christian Bible that will sooner or later work out the regeneration of our land."

The elevation of the outcastes The evidences of the loosening of the strangle-hold of caste have multiplied during the war. Many of these 53 million dispossessed working people of India went into the war. They came back with a vision of a new world. The upper classes were obliged to break caste regulations in the very act of crossing the seas and in the multitudinous contacts on the journey and in the field. They returned with a new vision. In no respect is the influence of the Bible to uplift whole communities more clearly seen than among these very outcaste Christians, who are "stepping down into Christianity," as the Hindus say, at the rate of ten thousand a month. When they become Christians,—poor and ignorant though they be—they begin to clean up.

When plague comes these simple Christians, freed from the base superstition of other outcastes, obey the sanitary rules given them by the missionaries, and excite the superstitious envy of their neighbors by their immunity from plague. In education, too, the change is marked. While the census of 1901 showed that among the whole 53 millions of outcastes only one-half of one percent were able to read, among the Christians the census of 1911 showed a higher percentage of literacy than even that of the Brahmins; the Christian percentage of literacy being 22 percent as compared with an average of 6 percent for all India. Yet 80 percent of the Christian population is made up of "untouchables." Another curious revelation of the fact that the Bible teaching does actually uplift socially and intellectually is that after becoming Christians, the "untouchables" are no longer considered "untouchables" in many parts of India. Some of their children even become teachers in caste schools; not a few gain university degrees.

The changing status of women According to the most revered and ancient Hindu laws, women are shut out from participation in social life, in religious privileges, in the kingdom of the mind. They are married in childhood, become mothers at the dawn of adolescence, and upon the death of their husbands are doomed to perpetual widowhood. During the hundred years in which India has been under the impact of Bible ideals these changeless customs and inhibitions affecting women have been silently undermined until today India is almost ready publicly to break with many customs long-buttressed by religion. Indian women are demanding education, are entering professional life, are coming out of their seclusion. There is not a department in their life unaffected by contact with Christian women of the West, and by the diffusion of the Christian Scriptures.

Uganda's marvelous transformation

Uganda is not only the scene of the most wonderful transformation of a whole people in all Africa, but one of the most wonderful in the whole world. Those who remember Stanley's description of the violence and evil which marked the life of the Baganda people, and his appeal for missionaries to their dark land can realize the miraculous change which has been effected in less than fifty years. From the days when King Mtesa wavered between belief and persecution, when the first Christian martyrs laid down their lives in flame and torture, when Bishop Hannington "opened the way to Uganda with his life," when Mackay toiled and Pilkington translated the Scripture is a time well within the memory of living men. Today the country is dotted with churches and school houses built and maintained by the people. There is a vast cathedral, the product of African workmanship and African gifts. In it a vested choir discourses sweet music, and great multitudes kneel in prayer. Missionaries drawn from the native church are freely supported among the heathen tribes. A constitutional monarchy with well-regulated laws has been established, and the prime minister, Apolo Kagwa, a black statesman, attended the coronation of Edward VII. Not only did he attend the coronation, but he wrote a delectable book about his experiences, on his return home, and multitudes of his country men bought it and read it. Uganda today is no savage wilderness. It has its railways, its harnessed waterpower, its post office and roads, its cultivated farms and neat homes. The Bible is the sole and sufficient cause of this transformation. There are other African tribes where trade has gone without the Bible and degraded the people even as it has purchased their goods. There are other peoples where European governments have taken control, only to ruin them. The missionary with his Bible got to Uganda, and got there first.

Jean Mackenzie in her *African Trail* recounts how the coming of the Bible begot confidence and mutual trust between suspicious tribes:

> Before the people of God began to spring up in the forest there was no intertribal talk of "brother" unless between allied tribes. I once heard long talk of this matter on a forest journey. I had four hammock carriers, each of a different tribe.
>
> "This walking that we walk today," they told each other on that journey, "is a strange walking for black people to walk; four men of four tribes walking in one company and doing one work. God alone could unite us after this fashion." And to the white woman they said, "Before the time of the things of God, not one of us but would have feared to meet the other. Ah, brothers, is it not a true word?"
>
> "He tells the truth!"
>
> "And now, we eat together and we sleep together like people of one village."

A story by David Livingstone

David Livingstone told how the teachers found the Sechuana Testament a powerful weapon. They said, "We thought it was a charm of the white people to ward off sickness, or that it was a trap to catch us. We had never heard of such a thing. Our fathers who have all died in the darkness could not tell us about it. We thought it was a thing to be spoken to; but now we know it has a tongue. It speaks and will speak to the whole world."

Hottentot testimony

In 1836 the wild men spoke for themselves in a great meeting in London, convened by the London Missionary Society. Said the Hottentot delegate: "When the Bible came to us we were naked; we lived in caves and on the tops of mountains; we painted our bodies with red paint. The Bible charmed us out of the caves and from the tops of the mountains. Now we know there is a God."

The Bible influences the Maoris

The influence of the Bible in transforming the island tribes of the Pacific has been marvelous. Maori soldiers have been among the best troops which New Zealand sent to the front in France. It is not three generations since their ancestors were naked savages. In 1839, without teacher or missionary, a solitary page of the catechism containing the Ten Commandments led one tribe to turn to the true God, to burn their idols, and to keep the Sabbath. One of the beautiful stories of those early days is of Tarore, the little daughter of Ngakuku, a converted chief. She always carried her father's copy of the Gospel of Luke, and, since she knew how to read, conducted the simple worship in her father's hut. At one time when he was traveling with an English party they halted for the night at Wairere, "flying water," and while they slept were attacked by a war party of the heathen. Ngakuku fled, carrying his little son, but in the confusion Tarore, sunk in sleep, was left behind. Her murderers carried off her gospel with the rest of the plunder. The robber chieftain read it, repented of his evil life, and longed to join the Christians. He wrote a letter to Ngakuku, asking permission to enter the chapel, and soon this Maori Christian and the murderer of his child "were worshipping God together in the same place," as the Maori story has it.

Charles Darwin testifies

Charles Darwin, the great naturalist, witnessed to the transformation which the Bible had wrought in Tahiti, one of the Society Islands, when he visited the island in the *Beagle* in 1835. When the missionaries landed at Tahiti in 1796, the islanders were sunk in incredible degradation. Constant war, shameless and bestial immorality, cruelty and superstition that descended to human sacrifice darkened the land and made life hideous. At first there seemed to be no higher self to appeal to; the soul of the people seemed seared as if with a branding iron of evil. But after heroic suffering and faithful witnessing to the truth on the part of the missionaries, they saw Ezekiel's miracle of the valley of the dry bones wrought once more. Mr. Darwin made an inland trip through the island where he had every opportunity to observe the natives in their daily life. He wrote:

> Before we laid ourselves down to sleep, the elder Tahitian fell on his knees, and with closed eyes repeated a long prayer in his native tongue. He prayed as a Christian should do, with fitting reverence, and without the fear of ridicule or any ostentation of piety. At our meals neither of the men would taste food without saying beforehand a short grace. Those travelers who think that a Tahitian prays only when the eyes of the missionary are fixed on him should have slept with us that night on the mountain." He goes on to discuss the rumor "that the

Tahitians had become a gloomy race, and lived in fear of the missionaries"; he says: "Of the latter feeling I saw no trace, unless, indeed, fear and respect be confounded under one name. Instead of discontent being a common feeling, it would be difficult in Europe to pick out of a crowd half so many merry and happy faces." He then replies to those who were ever ready to point out still existing defects in the South Sea Islanders, and blame the missionaries for these. He continues: "They forget, or will not remember, that human sacrifices and the power of an idolatrous priesthood, a system of profligacy unparalleled in any other part of the world, infanticide, a consequence of that system, bloody wars where the conquerors spared neither women nor children,—that all these have been abolished, and that dishonesty, intemperance, and licentiousness have been greatly reduced by the introduction of Christianity. In a voyager, to forget these things would be base ingratitude; for, should he chance to be on the point of shipwreck on some unknown coast, he will devoutly pray that the lesson of the missionary may have extended thus far."

Services of missionaries to Pacific Islanders

The influence of the missionaries, which is only that of the Bible incarnated in a human life, has been one of the strongest agencies acting in behalf of the child races of the Pacific Islands in opposition to cruel greed and oppression. They were American missionaries who exposed the infamies of the sandalwood trade and the kidnapping of islanders for forced work in South America. It was the missionary hero, Rev. John G. Paton, whose revelations of the iniquities of the liquor traffic in the South Seas induced the Congress of the United States and the governments of Europe to prohibit by international agreement the sale of liquor to these islanders.

It was James Chalmers, the Captain Greatheart of New Guinea, whose services made it possible for Great Britain to extend her sovereignty over a large part of New Guinea without bloodshed and with a scrupulous safeguarding of native rights never before known in such an agreement between white men and savages. Mr. Chalmers was cordially hated by land-grabbers and kidnappers of Kanaka labor. His influence with the government, because of his firsthand acquaintance with conditions gained by years of living among these men of the Stone Age was sufficient to get incorporated into, the government's plan of administration and treaty with the natives the prohibition of the importation of firearms, intoxicants, and explosives, the safeguarding of Kanaka labor, and the prohibition of the sale of land by a native to a white person. The commander of the British man-of-war who saw these chieftains trustingly affix their mark to papers whose contents they could not read, in sturdy confidence that "Tamate" would not betray them, had a new vision of the power of Christian leadership. When in 1886 this militant missionary spoke of his years among savages he uttered this ringing testimony regarding the Bible's power to change native races:

> I have had twenty-one years' experience among natives. I have seen the semicivilized and the uncivilized; I have lived with the Christian native and I have lived, dined, and slept with the cannibals. . . . For at least nine years of my life I have lived with the savages of New Guinea; but I have never yet met with a single man or woman, or a single people, that your civilization without Christianity has civilized. . . . Wherever there has been the slightest spark of civilization in the Southern Seas it has been because the gospel has been preached there, and wherever you find in the island of New Guinea a friendly people; there the missionaries of the Cross have been preaching Christ. Civilization! The rampart can only be stormed by those who carry the Cross.

Koreans, people of the Book

Korea is one of the outstanding instances of the transforming effect of the Bible. When Christianity entered in 1884, the whole people were sodden in superstition and spiritless from centuries of grinding between the upper and the nether millstones of China and Japan. The Korean government was a mixture of corruption and weakness. Of public spirit there was none visible. But the Koreans in multitudes have become people of the Book. They have supported their own churches and built them; they have sent their children to school and paid for their schooling. Of their language it can be said as was said of the Greek language, that it has "risen from the dead with the New Testament in its hand." Upon such a people, newly awakened from the sleep of centuries, Japan imposed a policy of forcible assimilation. There are new blood and iron in the soul of Korea to meet Japan's policy of "blood and iron." In a resistance devoid of violence, but full of quiet dignity and dauntless courage, Korea has appealed to that public opinion of the world which is itself the slow creation of the Bible's pressure upon the soul of humanity. The suffering of those who have died is not in vain. Korea in the might of meekness has saved her soul. All the generous elements in Japan have been stirred to shame as they have read the story of militarism's doings in Korea. Sooner or later Korea will win either her absolute freedom or such an honorable part in the empire of Japan as Canada has in the British empire. It will be the Bible's influence, the Bible that put a new soul into Korea, the Bible which is building up a new ideal in Japan.

Japan's debt to the Bible

The outstanding influence of Bible Christianity in Japan has been freely acknowledged by leading Japanese statesmen and thinkers. The words of Count Okuma, the prime minister, sum up testimonies that might be quoted from many others to like effect:

> Although Christianity has enrolled less than two hundred thousand believers yet the direct influence of Christianity has poured into every realm of Japanese life . . . Christianity has affected us not only in such superficial ways as the observance of Sunday, but also in our ideals concerning political institutions, the family, and woman's station. . . . Japan received Buddhism and Confucianism from India, China, and Korea, and under their influence she declined. But under the impact of Western Christianized thought Japan has revived.

The disproportionate influence of Christian Japanese on their government was clearly seen in the first Parliament of 1880, when out of three hundred members thirteen were Christian, including the speaker of the house. It is due to these outstanding Christians that the Bible's principles have gained recognition in the public life of Japan.

Christian music in Japan

The music of Christianity has profoundly modified the music of Japan. When the missionaries first began to teach the children to sing it was thought that a special scale would have to be invented to fit the Japanese voice. Today Japanese choruses render the great chorals of the Christian faith, and the Union Christian hymnal is one of the best selling books in Japan.

Improved status of women

The Bible teachings have already profoundly modified the position of the Japanese women. A new sacredness is accorded to marriage. From the empress to the humblest of her subjects all Japanese women are indebted to Christianity for their improved status. Christians have been the leaders in the determined war against government-recognized prostitution, as they have in the organized struggle against intemperance.

Christian influence in prison reform

Prison reform in Japan received impetus in 1875 when Dr. J. C. Berry secured permission to make a tour of inspection of the prisons. His report led directly to prison reform throughout the empire. For this service he was years later presented with an Imperial Decoration. One of the immediate effects was the appointment of a Christian as chaplain in the prison in Kobe. As a result of his teachings eight prisoners formed themselves into "The Company of the Covenant." Later the chaplain became superintendent and continued his blessed work. It was at about this time that a group of eighty convicts were reading Martin's *Evidences of Christianity,* which an educated fellow-prisoner was translating for them into Japanese. When fire broke out in the prison they put out the flames and created no disorder. Their leader was pardoned and later started a private school in Otsu.

Japanese Christians influential

When the history of Japan during the last thirty years is studied it will be found that behind her wonderful achievement there has usually been someone, Japanese or foreigner, whose torch has been kindled by the light of the world. Although numbering only one-half of one percent of the population, the Christians of Japan are influential in all that shapes her higher life. In her public schools, her new philanthropy, her growing recognition of the *human* rights of her citizens, in the currents of democracy now running silently but nonetheless strongly, Japan is influenced by the nations most deeply influenced by the Bible.

During the present trouble in Korea, Japanese Christians have been fearless critics of the militaristic elements in their own government. Professor Nitobe, president of the newly established Christian College for Women in Tokyo, has boldly condemned his country's policy in Korea. Rev. Takashi Suzuki published in the Fukuin Shimpo, May 15, 1919, an article amazing in its frank recognition of evils and injustices in the Japanese policy in Korea. The article has been translated into English and reprinted in the September number of *The Missionary Review of the World.* It should be read by anyone who desires to measure the force exerted in Japanese life by the Christian conceptions of right and duty. It is to be doubted whether America or England could show a finer example of the functioning of the Christian conscience on public questions.

Bible influence in the opening of China

The clearest illustration of the influence of the Bible upon a great non-Christian nation is China. That influence is to be traced to the very beginnings of modern intercourse with China. The first treaty negotiated with America, in 1844, was accomplished through the services of Rev. E. C. Bridgman and Dr. Peter Parker, two men who in obedience to the Bible had left home and country and become Chinese to the Chinese, that they might win them to Christ. Their knowledge of the people and the language, and the confidence which the Chinese felt toward them were "simply invaluable," said the Hon. Caleb Cushing, that noble Christian statesman. It was this great American minister who secured in the treaty a clause prohibiting all traffic in opium between the two countries. The Chinese have long memories for this truly Christian service. It was through the medium of Morrison and Gützlaff that England negotiated her first treaty.

Services of American missionaries

In the historic treaty of 1858 two American missionaries rendered notable services to China, and the world. Dr. S. Wells Williams and Dr. W. A. P. Martin were the men who secured the first toleration clause which China had ever granted in any treaty. The far-reaching influence of this clause makes it a Magna Charta in the story of Chinese freedom of thought and action. Dr. Williams, to whose persistency, tact, and statesmanship the greatest credit is due for this achievement, became interpreter to the United States Legation in Peking, and so remained until 1876. The Hon. W. B. Reed, who was the American Minister to China when the treaty was negotiated, said: "Without them (Williams and Martin) public business could not be transacted. I could not but for their aid have advanced one step in the discharge of my duties here." It was S. Wells Williams who later, at the request of Commodore Perry, helped to negotiate the first treaty with Japan.

Christian diplomacy in China

Not only have American missionaries deeply influenced the progress of the Chinese nation, but American diplomats, as well. Anson Burlingame, American Minister to China, was no less missionary because he represented the American nation. The golden rule diplomacy of John Hay was the very genius of the New Testament in action. The Chinese can never forget that it was American Christianity and not American gunboats that saved her integrity when Hay challenged the moral sense of the world in behalf of the integrity of China and in opposition to schemes of selfish aggrandizement.

The Bible in the imperial palace An interesting story of the way in which the Bible was brought to bear on persons of the highest influence in the Chinese government comes from the days of the Empress Dowager in 1896.

The Christian women of China decided to present a Bible to her majesty on the occasion of her sixtieth birthday. They contributed $600 in gold, ten thousand of them uniting in the gift. For the first time a Chinese Bible penetrated into the imperial palace, when the empress received the sumptuously bound and printed volume. Two days later the Chief Eunuch from the palace was sent out to buy a Bible and all the Christian books he could get for the emperor. The full account of this visit of the eunuch is found in Dr. Hykes' pamphlet *The American Bible Society in China* (Centennial pamphlet no. 12, pp. 25–26). Following this first order for books, in 1897 the Emperor sent for a list of one hundred and forty books, some scientific, but many religious. Among these books were commentaries on the books of the Bible, *The Life of Christ, Benefits of Christianity, Communion with God*, and four sermons by Mr. Moody. The effect of this sending for Christian books by the emperor was plainly seen in the greatly increased sales of the Scriptures. There is little doubt that the young emperor in his inexperience and his new hope for his country was influenced by his reading to put forth his ill-fated edicts for reform the following year. The reactionary Empress Dowager could not destroy his proposed reforms, though she did delay them and destroy the emperor. Many of his reforms are already established, others are on the way.

Testimony of a Chinese philanthropist In making one of his presentations of Bibles to the gentry to which allusion has already been made, Mr. Yung Tao, the Chinese philanthropist, said:

> Without the aid of Christian ethics it is impossible to reform society or to expel evil from men's hearts so as to produce a *strong and virtuous nation*. Many people believe that God has so miraculously preserved China for thousands of years because he has some great future for her. It may be. I do not know. But I believe my country has reached the supreme crisis in her history. The next few years will determine

> whether she is to have a great and useful future or is doomed to extinction. If she is to endure she must accept the teachings of the Bible. It is only by accepting the true God and fulfilling duty to him that a nation can endure.

When later Mr. Yung Tao became a Christian, he spoke of the missionaries as follows:

> Who loves China? The Chinese people? No! The merchants? No! The diplomats? No! Only the missionaries, who come here not asking to be paid, but asking to be allowed merely to work for China.

Christian education back of influential Chinese

In every part of Chinese life you can trace the influence of the Book. When the decree establishing Western education was made, missionaries were asked to become the heads of government schools and colleges. Mission-trained men leaped into positions of influence. If you were to name the twenty men most prominent in Chinese affairs today, it would be safe to hazard the guess that two-thirds of them received their first education in mission schools. The three men who represented China at the Peace Conference were the products of Christian education,—two of them, certainly, outstanding Christians.

Influence of one Christian college

St. John's College, Shanghai, is a notable example of the influence which Christian education has exerted on the national awakening of the Chinese. Although the school was established in 1879, it did not develop into a college until late in the nineties. From that time until June 1917, it had graduated but two hundred and eighteen men. From this small group have come twelve men of national or international significance. They include Dr. W. W. Yen, late Minister to Germany; Dr. V. K. Wellington Koo, Minister to the United States and one of China's three representatives to the Peace Conference; Dr. Y. T. Tsur, president of Tsing Hwa, the indemnity college; Dr. Z. T. K. Woo, superintendent of the Hanyang Iron and Steel Works, one of the greatest steel plants in the East; Mr. S. C. Chu, general secretary of the Shanghai-Nanking Railroad; the late Mr. T. T. Wang, director general of the Chinese Students' Educational Commission at Washington, D.C.; Dr. Hawkling L. Yen, secretary of the Board of Foreign Affairs; Mr. David Z. T. Yui, general secretary of the Chinese Y.M.C.A.; Rev. P. N. Tsu, rector of the Church of Our Savior;

Dr. Yen Fu Ching, dean of the medical faculty of Yale College in China, and Judge W. Y. Hu, justice of the Supreme Court of Appeals, Peking.

High officials cable American Bible Society

During the celebration of the American Bible Society, held in connection with the Methodist Centenary at Columbus, Ohio, last June, cable messages were received from some of China's most powerful leaders, among them the president of the Republic. Wen Shih Tsin, commissioner of foreign affairs, cabled: "Darkness and gloom reign in China. The Bible is the only remedy by which we will save China, cure the corrupt officials and heal the ambitious politicians, inspire the educators and uplift the poor; and the best of all is to tell our people how to do righteousness and sacrifice for our own nation."

Message of a great educator

A distinguished educator, Yu-Yue Tsu, sent his message in English, as follows: "The translation of the Christian Bible into our national language has placed in the hands of our people a book than which there is none with greater power for moral uplift and spiritual enlightenment. The great ideas of divine love, human brotherhood, holiness, unselfish service, all culminating in the wonderful ideal of the kingdom of God on earth, are emphasized and exemplified in its pages as nowhere else. They are powerful dynamics in undoing social wrongs and erasing class distinctions, in humanizing social relationships and democratizing governments. They have condemned the opium traffic, raised the status of women and children, purified the home, emancipated the slaves, energized the moral nature of humanity, taught the value of human life, produced happiness in life and labor, and created a new conscience both for the individual and for the community. The open Bible, the greatest heritage of Christendom, is now made accessible to China's millions, and it will not fail as their guide and inspirer in the nation's upward struggle for moral, perfection and spiritual freedom."

Message of China's president

The president of the Republic of China cabled as follows: "The instruction concerning all virtue, as contained in the Holy Scriptures of the religion of Jesus, has truly exerted an unlimited influence for good among all Christians in China, and has also raised the standard of all my people along lines of true progress. I earnestly hope that the future benefits derived from the Holy Scriptures will extend to the ends of the earth and transcend the success of the past."

The Chinese government asks Christians to pray

One of the most dramatic indications of the influence exerted by the gospel upon the national life of China was given on April 19, 1913. The cabinet of the Chinese government adopted on that day the following message, which was ordered to be sent to the provincial authorities and to the leaders of the Christian church in China:

> Prayer is requested for the National Assembly now in session; for the new Government; for the President who is to be elected; for the Constitution of the Republic; that the Government may be recognized by the powers; that peace may reign within our country; that strong and virtuous men may be elected to office; and that the Government may be established upon a strong foundation. Upon receipt of this telegram you are requested to notify all churches in your province that April twenty-seventh has been set aside as a day of prayer for the nation. Let all take part.

Not only was this day of prayer ordered, it was widely observed not only by Christian believers but by leading officials, provincial and national.

The Bible going back home again

It is an astounding fact that the great non-Christian nations of the world have been in league with Christian nations in defense of a cause whose taproot is the Bible. Outside of nations under the tutelage of the Bible there is not one which has ever grasped the first meanings of democracy. The nations are looking to one standard. They are seeing that there is but one help out of their present distresses. Fresh light is waiting to break out of the holy page—the only source whence light can come. "Our Bible, our Christ, our alphabet" came from the Orient. Today the Orient, by train and steamer, is coming to us to get back her own. A great sense of commonalty is in the air. Converging from every nation men are walking on paths that lead to the Holy City coming down from God out of heaven, and to that united humanity which has washed its robes and made them white in the blood of the Lamb.

> "A glory gilds the sacred page, Majestic like the sun;
>
> * * * * *
>
> Its truths upon the nations rise, They rise and set no more."

Outline
Chapter 6

I. In Christian Lands Literary Influence of Bible Seen
   1. In Stimulating of books and libraries
   2. In permeation of literature in style and substance
   3. In impression made by English literature on non-Christians
   4. In impossibility of effacing its mark

II. Introduction of Bible into non-Christian Lands Produces:
   1. A literate Christian community
   2. Preparation of school textbooks
   3. Introduction and development of printing press (notable presses)
   4. Agencies for preparation and distribution of Christian literature

III. Study of Christian Literature
   1. The tract societies
   2. Christian literature societies; illustration: work of Christian Literature Society of China

IV. Stimulation of Literary Activities in non-Christian Lands
   1. Writings of Japanese Christians
      a. Translation
      b. Original works
      c. Illustration, Japan
   2. Christward currents in writings of non-Christians
   3. Gospel influence in the daily press

4. Advertising Christianity in the newspapers

V. Influence of the Bible on Music in non-Christian Lands

1. Christianity's gift of song
2. The missionary and his hymnal
3. The popularity of Christian hymn books
4. Oriental hymn writers: Indian

VI. Unmet Needs for Christian Literature

1. Literature for the home
   Needs of women
   Needs of children
   Illustration, *Child's Life of Jesus*
   Children's magazine, *Happy Childhood*
2. Periodical literature
   Needs of cooperative publishing
3. An adequate program
   Expense of program

VII. Outstanding Opportunities for Advance

1. United Campaign of newspaper publicity
2. Utilization of phonetic script in China
   Its importance and advantages, overcoming Chinese conservatism
   America's possible contribution in printing textbooks
   Opportunity for the Christian Church

VIII. Conclusion

Six

The Leaves of the Tree

The mere ethical teachings of the bible would alone stamp it as the greatest literary treasure of humanity.

Goethe

A Book-making Book

"The Bible is a book-making Book. It is literature which provokes literature," says McAfee in *The Greatest English Classic.* The statement is so overwhelmingly true that it is difficult to illustrate it within the sharp limits of the present chapter. No race, for example, has ever read the Bible without an irresistible desire to write about it. A flood of sermons, treatises, histories, biographies, geographies, books of travel, theologies, philosophies, criticisms, defenses, dictionaries, encyclopedias, novels, poems, has flowed from under its portals like the river in Ezekiel's vision which from a rivulet became a torrent, waters to swim in, a river that could not be passed over. Nor is there any sign of an abatement in interest. Apparently the perennial interest of the Scripture demands that each generation wrestle afresh with its problems and afresh record its poignant reactions to the stimulus of the Book.

Output of books greatest in Christendom

This book-germinating influence of the Bible is marked when we compare the output of books on the part of nations longest under the Christian discipline with those longest under that of other great world religions. In no one of the Oriental nations is the output of books comparable to that in Christian nations. During the last half century or more in which the ferment of the gospel has been actively at work in nations like India, China, and Japan, the effect upon the writing of books, as well as upon political and social institutions, has been clearly seen. In Oriental nations, like Tibet and Turkestan, and in Morocco, as yet virtually closed to the Bible, conditions remain such as they were in the entire Orient when the era of modern missions began. Furthermore, the accessibility of the Bible and its wide diffusion among the people of Christian nations seem to be in direct relation to the amount and quality of the literary output.

Christianity develops a book-reading public

Take for example matter of public libraries as it is so strikingly brought out in President Tenney's *Contrasts in Social Progress.* He says:

> There is no point of difference between Christian and non-Christian literature more notable than that relating to the popularization of books. The Turkish Empire would have today ten millions of books in local libraries, scattered here and there in different cities and towns, if Islam favored popular education by literature as much as Christianity did in Great Britain in 1880. Take Persia, where the people are nearly all Mohammedans; that kingdom would have today eight hundred libraries with six and a quarter millions of books in them, if their religion favored popular reading as much as Christianity in the United States. Two hundred millions of books would be upon the shelves of native libraries in India open to the reading of all castes, if Brahmanism were the match of Christianity in America for diffusing education by books. Here is Buddhism; there ought to be more than thirty-five hundred libraries here and there in Japan, with almost thirty millions of volumes in them, and there ought to be more than ten millions of books in the native libraries of Ceylon, Siam, and Burma today, if their faith were as good a popular educator by books as Christianity is today in the United States. China, the most literary of the non-Christian nations, has no books to speak of, aside from one library of one hundred and sixty-eight thousand volumes, and small libraries in the eighteen provinces, and little gatherings of books in the Buddhist monasteries; but if Confucianism were as good a patron

of books as Christianity in America, there would be in the Celestial Kingdom today more than twenty-nine thousand libraries, each averaging eighty-five hundred volumes. *Christianity is a reading religion.* When Saul, in the old story, saw any strong man, or any valiant man, he took him unto himself. *Strong and valiant books are in demand throughout Christendom. The mighty men of valor are the men of ideas.*

The Book permeates literature Not only is it true that the Bible breeds books about itself, and develops a book-reading people; the Book also enters into and permeates the literature of Christian peoples. This is true in English literature to an extent little dreamed of. We are so accustomed to the fact that we fail to realize its significance. The very titles of the books we read are redolent of the Bible. A few examples may be given, taken quite at random from the multitude that might be cited. Mrs. Wharton's *House of Mirth,* Basil King's *Graham's Bosom,* Rupert Hughes' *The Unpardonable Sin,* Ibanez' *The Four Horsemen of the Apocalypse,* are a few current titles. Dipping into the past we recall Ruskin's *Crown of Wild Olives, Unto this Last, Seven Lamps of Architecture,* Milton's *Paradise Lost, Samson Agonistes,* Byron's *Jephtha's Daughter, Cain,* Browning's *Bells and Pomegranates, Saul, Easter Morning, Christmas Eve,* Dryden's *Absalom and Achitophel,* Whittier's *Ichabod.* If we turn from titles to substance we go from the shallows to the deep sea. Dr. Furnivall says that "Shakespeare is saturated with the Bible story." Milton is scriptural in the very fabric of his diction. *The Pilgrim's Progress* is compounded of biblical phraseology and ideas. From it Thackeray drew the title of his *Vanity Fair,* though he took the motto of the book directly from the Bible. The biblical phrases, quotations, and allusions in Browning are so numerous as to obscure his thought to one not familiar with the Bible. Some one has counted five hundred such in *The Ring and the Book* alone, McAfee tells us. Longfellow's most exquisite metaphors and similes are taken bodily from the Bible. VanDyke has found four hundred direct references to the Bible in Tennyson, and that leaves out those subtler echoes and nuances with which his pages are so full that no one whose mind is not steeped in the Bible can really appreciate him. Ruskin is a classic illustration of a literary style formed on the Bible. Familiarity with the Bible is stamped on the pages of Scott, Dickens, Macaulay, Lowell, Whittier, and a score of other names familiar wherever English and American books are read. Even writers avowedly out of sympathy with the Bible cannot avoid indebtedness to it, as for example, Shelley, when he writes, "Their errors have been weighed and found to have been dust in the balance; If their sins are scarlet, they are now white as snow, they have been washed in the blood of the mediator and redeemer, Time." On one editorial page of a recent number of *Collier's Weekly* the following Bible phrases or allusions were found: "Hiram, King of Tyre"; "Go down to the sea in ships"; "Six days shalt thou labor"; "And they shall teach no more everyone their neighbor."

English literature interprets Christianity to Japan

The realization of this saturation of English literature with the Bible came with poignancy to an American college woman who, while spending a winter in Tokyo, was asked to fill temporarily a vacancy which had been caused by death in the faculty of the Peeresses School. She said to a friend later, "Until those eager girls asked me, day after day, to explain the meaning of this figure of speech or that phrase or that allusion or proper name, I had no idea of the way that the Bible entered into the very structure of our literature." Professor Nitobe of the Imperial University in Tokyo has testified that it was the indirect presentation of Christian truth through works of English literature during a period in which he had denied to the missionaries any access to his soul, that led him to accept the Christian faith.

Impossibility of blotting out Bible influence

The all-penetrating influence of the Bible on modern literature may be realized by an attempt to root it out, we should need to burn all Bibles. Testaments, and hymn books; then to mutilate every law book and commentary; to black out page after page in the works of the poets and to destroy entire books whose titles were biblical. Hardly a novel of any standing would remain intact. The essays, histories, and biographies would be sadly mutilated. The works of Huxley, Tyndall, Spencer, and other scientists would not escape the tearing out of no inconsiderable portions. The greatest works of music would perish. The masterpieces of painting and sculpture would be defaced or destroyed. The most sublime buildings of Europe and America would need to be dynamited. Into every cemetery the iconoclast would go to chisel from the tombs the words of hope. The motto would need to be chipped from the walls of the Harvard Law School and from the great seal of this and other universities. Not a library could escape unscathed; not a church building be left standing. When all this were done the Bible would remain indestructible in the memory of living men. To say nothing of Western nations, there are school children in China and Japan who can repeat the entire New Testament from memory. There are not a few Scotch Christians who have committed the Psalms and Isaiah to memory. It is perfectly within the bounds of fact to assert that in some heart each portion of Scripture is cherished, so that it could be reproduced were the printed record lost. To destroy the influence of the Bible it would be necessary to massacre every Christian, and even this would not be enough, for in their death they would surely repeat some precious word that could be erased from the memory of their murderers no more readily than could Paul forget Stephen's face and Stephen's dying prayer.

The Bible transplanted creates demand for books

Dealing with such a book we may naturally expect that the result of its planting in non-Christian lands has fruited in a new love and a new demand for Christian books. The tree of the gospel planted in the garden of human life canopies itself with leaves that are the healing of the nations.

(1) By creating a literate constituency

The Bible creates a hunger for books by producing a generation of readers. The idea of putting the tool of literacy in the hands of common men is itself an offshoot of democracy which is the creation of Christianity. All the so-called democracies of ancient times were in truth democracies within the crassest class oligarchies. The conception of one body politic, social, religious, for all humanity, is born of the teaching and life of Jesus, and is yet to be fully recognized even in nations calling themselves Christian. It is then to be expected that only in nations where the common people are recognized as having some share and stake in government has the experiment of universal education been attempted. Japan, the one seeming exception, is none in reality, since Japan transplanted the idea bodily from Christian countries. When Christian missionaries go to a new land, they carry the Bible as the vehicle for their message. They are forced to begin to teach people to read in order that the Bible may convey the message. This leads to the turning out from the Christian schools in every land multitudes of potential readers every year.

(2) By preparation of textbooks

In setting up this institution for teaching the revolutionary art of reading, the missionaries have carried on other educational enterprises. Reading, writing, and arithmetic, not to mention other subjects, have all had to be taught. This has meant in many cases the forming of the tools of education in process of setting up the schools. One effect of taking the Bible to non-Christian lands has been to plunge the missionaries into the task of writing school textbooks. It is safe to say that the bulk of the spellers, readers, arithmetics, geographies, and histories introduced into Asia during the nineteenth century were the work of missionaries or their pupils. To take but two illustrations out of a multitude: In Burma, in 1913, one of the numerous editions of Stillman's *Arithmetic* was going through the press at Rangoon. So closely did this pioneer missionary of two generations past fit his presentations and examples of arithmetical truth to Burmese life that no later arithmetic has been able to replace it in the schools of Burma. The *School History of Egypt* in use in government schools was written by a Christian Egyptian woman, the first of the nation to receive a college degree in the Woman's Christian College of Cairo.

(3) By creation of new industries

The preparation or translation of text of books by the missionaries for their Christian schools led to the creation of new industries. Sometimes rude printing presses and fonts of type were laboriously improvised by the missionaries, as in the case of John Williams in the South Seas or William Duncan among the Cree Indians. More often printing presses were imported and the natives taught to run them. The superhuman efforts necessary to procure or manufacture proper type and get a press actually in operation are one of the romances of missions.

Notable missionary presses

Notable missionary presses are the Baptist Press at Rangoon, where the Bibles, Christian literature, and many of the educational books for polyglot Burma have been printed for the last seventy-five years; the Methodist Episcopal Press at Lucknow, with about two hundred employees and an annual output of 74,600,000 pages; the Presbyterian Mission Press at Beirut, where the Bible for 200 million Moslems and a large proportion of all the Arabic textbooks of the world are printed. There are more than one hundred and sixty mission presses in the different fields, scattered among the societies of all denominations. Some of them are busy little presses like that at Goom on the borders of Tibet, where the Scandinavian Alliance Mission is printing Bibles to smuggle into that closed land. Others are great business enterprises like the Presbyterian Press at Shanghai. It was a group of young Chinese Christians trained in this press who organized the Commercial Press, Limited, of Shanghai. Beginning in a small way, this publishing house is today the largest in all Asia. It is equipped with the most modern presses, imports paper stock from Austria, Sweden, England, and Japan, and prints two-thirds of the textbooks of China. Best of all, this firm is thoroughly Christian, with standards in regard to sanitary conditions, wages, and welfare work that would put to shame all but the most advanced business concerns of the West.

Work of tract societies

To meet the growing demand for books created by the missionary schools, special societies have been organized, such as the American Tract Society and the Christian Literature Societies of India, China, and Japan. The work of the tract societies is a romance by itself. A tract is the outward and visible budding of a growing cause. Whether political, scientific, or religious, all causes are alike in this, that they inevitably break into tracts—a sort of hand-clapping to attract attention. Neither should the tract be despised because of its ephemeral nature and humble form. Tracts are the true stuff out of which revolutions are built. The big books move too slowly to catch the crowd. Elaborate explanations prove exhausting to the attention of the unthinking. A tract catches the eye of the person as they run, finds them as they rest by the way, speaks to them in the homely colloquial of their daily speech. The Religious Tract Society of London and the American Tract Society stand in the same relation to the production and distribution of tracts as do the British and Foreign Bible Society and the American Bible Society to the circulation of the Bible.

Christian Literature Society of China

The Christian Literature Societies' aim is other than that of the tract society. Their field is education rather than propaganda. Recognizing the keen hunger for books on the part of the awakening nations of the East, they seek to meet it by making available the riches of the Christian literature of the West through translation and by stimulating the development of native literature. One of the most remarkable of these societies is the Christian Literature Society of China. After the death of its founder Dr. Alexander Williamson in 1891, Rev. Timothy Richard, a Welsh Baptist missionary, became the secretary of the society. Under his dynamic leadership the organization became one of the mightiest powers in the transformation of China. Beginning with assets of only $1,000, he drew about him a splendid body of Chinese and European editors and translators, accumulated property for the Society to the value of

$22,000 and poured forth an ever increasing flood of life-giving books into the mud; stretches of the national life. He was known throughout China by the Chinese version of his given name, Teem-o-ti. The emperor, in recognition of his great services, ennobled him ancestors for three generations (an attention peculiarly treasured by the Chinese), and made Dr. Richard himself Mandarin with the button of the highest grade.

Timothy Richard's great achievement

Dr. Richard was one of the first to see the strategic importance of books awakening the mighty Chinese nation from its sleep. He translated the word *Christian* in no narrow way, but in addition to books of devotion and biblical exposition published works of the widest range of interest. A little of the scope of the Society's work may be understood by listing a few titles: *International Law, The German Empire, Sixty Years of Queen Victoria, Life of Luther, Biographic Sketches of the Presidents* of *the United States,* Guizot's *History of European Civilization, Tea Cultivation Science and Alcohol, The Romance of Medicine, History of Western Ethics, Outlines of Astronomy, Political Economy, History of Socialism, Primer of Sanitation, Physical Education, Training of Children.* In all his provision for adults, the children were not forgotten, as witness the translation of *Little Fauntleroy.*

Christian books for Kuang Hsu

When the young emperor sent his eunuchs for books, he had to depend chiefly upon the Christian Literature Society for those dealing with the history and civilization of Western nations. Among others he received Mackenzie's *History of the Nineteenth Century.* The Russian ambassador was quite naturally shocked when he learned that the young emperor was deeply impressed by the book. He warned the emperor of its dangerous quality, and thus succeeded in bringing the book to the attention of one of the viceroys, who in turn was so impressed that he presented a copy to the viceroys of the seventeen other Chinese provinces. In presenting the book he urged them to read it, saying that a civilization that could make such an advance in one century was one of which China could not afford to be ignorant.

Wide branching topics of Christian literature

Through literally hundreds of similar illustrations which might be given, it is clearly evident that forces liberated in the bringing of the Bible to China have been at the very heart of the momentous changes taking place in that country during the last quarter century. The number of distinctively religious books and pamphlets published by the society is very great, and ranges from a translation of Hastings' Bible dictionary to a series of large and attractive posters printed in red with the flag of the Republic reproduced in colors. The posters deal with religion in relation to the State, Education, and the Home. A life of Christ, notes on the Sermon on the Mount, church history, object lessons for children, studies in the New Testament, Christianity and civil government are a few of the wide-branching topics on which Chinese Christians desire to be informed.

Christian periodical literature

Not least important among the activities of the society is the publication of periodical literature. The one magazine for women discusses topics so familiar to American women in their own similar magazines—home making, child training, child psychology, school sanitation, kindergarten games, etc., etc. The department of poetry contains translations from well-known English poems as well as original matter. Bible lessons, devotional pages, travel talks, sketches of famous women make up a magazine that is a boon to Chinese women, as it is the only publication of the sort in China.

First Chinese Christian newspaper

The growing power and self-consciousness of the Chinese Church were shown in 1912 in the establishment of the first Christian daily newspaper in China, *Great Light Daily*, edited by Mr. Leang Chi Sheng.

First magazine for children

The Christian Literature Society has the further distinction of publishing *Happy Childhood,* the only children's magazine in the Chinese language. That the magazine is appreciated is shown by the fact that its subscribers are found in all classes, in every province in China, and also in Hawaii, Malaysia, the Philippines, America, and in England, where there are Chinese children.

Literary output of Japanese Christians: translations

There is no non-Christian land where the output of Christian books is larger or more influential than in Japan. Japanese Christians are busily translating a multitude of useful books. Simpson's *Fact of Christ,* Anderson's *Man of Nazareth,* J. R. Miller's *Story of Joseph,* biographies of Moody and Judson, Fosdick's *The Meaning of Prayer,* Tolstoi's *My Religion*, Gordon's *Quiet talks on Prayer,* Bowne's *Theism,* Smiles' *Self Help,* Miss Porter's *Pollyanna,* and Wallace's *Ben Hur* are a few of those mentioned in the report of 1917.

Literary output of Japanese Christians: original works

Japanese Christians are writing books of their own, too. Mr. Horlguchi wrote a volume of studies in the Minor Prophets, Mr. Kuranaga, *Fifty Studies in the Gospel of John,* Mr. Kamizawa, a *Life of Christ,* Col. Yamamuro of the Salvation Army, a *Life of Christ in Common Speech.* Sixty-one thousand copies of this author's *The Gospel for the Common People* have been sold. There are books on the Holy Land, the life of St. Paul, sermons, lectures, essays, stories for young people, books on Sunday school organization, and teaching, and devotional books. A notable one among the latter class was *Under the Shadow of Thy Wings* (to translate its Japanese title) by Miss Zako Aiko. The author is an invalid, suffering much in body but triumphant in soul. Her brief essays are described as "prose poems" likely to become classics in their ministry of cheer to the suffering. Professor Tsunajima of Waseda University, after losing his faith, recovered it when he gained a new vision of God during a time of illness. His book *The Experience of Seeing God* has explained the meaning of faith to multitudes.

Christian literature outside the church

There are deep, Christward currents in Japan as in other countries which run outside the church. One evidence of this is found in the books written by those who are not avowed Christians. Tolstoi's writings have exerted a great influence in Japan through the translation of his complete works. There are Tolstoi clubs among students and a magazine devoted to the discussion and interpretation of his writings. "*Resurrection* has appeared everywhere in moving pictures," says *The Christian Movement in Japan,* 1919, "and has exerted an unquestioned influence for good among wide classes of society. The prayer to God of the heroine, Katuscha, sung by thousands in Japan, is part of the story of Nebdorf's repentance and experience of Christ's resurrection." Another book mentioned is *Go Go no Haru* (*The Spring of Five Times Five*), a book by a young writer named Kawano, which has had a profound effect upon the student world. Although Kawano never entered a Christian church he bought a penny Testament which he read while a student at Waseda University. In his book, which has sold by the tens of thousands, he tells of the blessing he received from his little Testament, eulogizes its power, and speaks of Christ and the Sermon on the Mount.

Buddhist approaches

The influence of the Bible can be traced in books even further removed from organic Christianity than the above.

Some of the leaders of new Buddhism frankly appropriate some of the leading ideas of Christianity. Idolatry is abolished and the movement leans toward Christianity with no sense of antagonism. One group of Buddhist ascetics has taken the Lord's Prayer as its motto. Two recent books of essays are listed by *The Christian Movement in Japan,* 1919, as "essentially Christian," i.e., books that could not have been written apart from the impact of Bible ideals and teachings upon the soul of Japan. *Cain and His Descent* by Arishima and *New Spring* by Tokutomi are the two books mentioned. The latter, which is a record of profoundly Christian experiences, passed through a hundred and four editions in less than one year.

The gospel in the daily press A touch of interest is added to the story of the slow but sure penetrations of Christian ideals into Japan through the printed pages to read that one newspaper ran as a serial a translation of Mrs. Stowe's *A Minister's Wooing* for the purpose of giving a picture of the religious life in New England of the long ago. A Tokyo newspaper ran the *Life of Christ* in serial form a few years ago; and an Osaka newspaper ran two prize novels as serials. Both were by Christian writers, one of them dealing with the power of prayer.

Advertising Christianity in the newspapers One of the most hopeful developments has been the utilizing of the daily press for the spread of Christian truth by means of paid advertising. The project was conceived by Rev. Albertus Pieters of Oita who began some years ago to explain the fundamental teachings of Christianity in the daily press. Readers of his masterly advertisements were told that they could secure further literature by writing to him. They were also invited to ask questions. His experiment disclosed how far these newspapers circulated, as letters began to reach him from widely separated localities. A careful card index of inquirers was made and a systematic follow-up work of correspondence began.

Results of gospel advertising The results of this campaign of gospel advertising have been surprisingly good. The prefecture of Oita, in which Dr. Pieters has been demonstrating his method of gospel seed-sowing through the medium of daily papers, has a population of 900,000. After several years of such cultivation the statement is boldly made that there is not a hamlet containing twenty houses in the entire prefecture, in which someone does not know the outstanding facts of the gospel.

> One Episcopal worker whose duties take him over large parties of Oita prefecture declares that he has no words to describe what this work has done, both in arousing interest among non-Christians and in nourishing the faith of scattered Christians. A pastor of the Reformed Church of over ten years' experience in the prefecture declares the change beyond imagining.

Expansion of newspaper advertising

Convinced that there are great possibilities of usefulness in the enlarged use of the newspapers as a medium of spreading the gospel, Dr. Pieters has organized an Association for the Promotion of Newspaper Evangelism. He is showing that at far smaller expense a larger number of people can be reached through the newspapers than through the distribution of tracts. He proposes that the Christian bodies engaged in missionary work in Japan shall raise a fund of $250,000 to carry newspaper evangelism into every corner of the empire. He suggests that Japanese Christians such as Mr. Kanamori, Col. Yamamuro, and Mr. Mitami be engaged to write in the simple, stirring style which they command, the vital truths of the gospel. A fund like this, available each year, would carry the gospel within twenty years into the remotest corners of the empire. The good idea is spreading into other lands, is to be tried, it is said, by the China Continuation Committee, by Mr. MacLeod in Formosa, and Dr. Zwemer in Egypt.

Publish glad tidings

Possibilities of tremendous good are opened up. It was the Bible that bade us lift up our voices and cry aloud and tell out among the people the glorious news of the gospel. Too often the news has been whispered or droned or repeated lifelessly in a corner. The wonderful publicity program of the government during the great war has proved that it is as easy to sell ideas to the people as to sell goods, if it is attempted in the right way, on a proper scale. Why is it not possible, in America, as well as in the Orient, to utilize the newspapers in merchandising wisdom? Why could not the National Chamber of Commerce through a worthy campaign of advertising in Japanese newspapers sell America to the Japanese,—to use an advertising term? The papers of Japan are flooded with malicious rumors about America's sinister designs on Japan: why not give them an advertising campaign of truth?

The singing leaves One of the loveliest legacies of the Book is the gift of song. Music there is in every land, but the soul of music has never found itself except under the culture of Christianity. The music of Greece, of India, of China remained primitive, plaintive, undeveloped. No religion except Christianity has ever been able so to develop personality as to bring out the hidden sublimities and marvelous possibilities that dwell in the soul of music. Wherever the Bible has gone the people have learned a new song.

The missionaries and their hymnals Missionaries have always taken their hymn books with their Bibles. The gospel has literally sung its way around the world. Simple hymns like *Safe in the Arms of Jesus, Jesus Loves Me, This I Know* are imperishably fixed in all earth's hundreds of languages. Some of our notable writers will be forgotten in a hundred years, but Fanny Crosby will go singing down the century. Hers was but a slender gift of song, but she placed it in the hands of Jesus and he blessed and broke and gave it to the nations. Missionary after missionary has translated and written hymns by the score to make the first crude hymnal of the newborn churches of the Orient. Time would fail to speak of the *Choice Arabic Hymns* first published by Rev. E. R. Lewis, M.D., a professor in the Syrian Protestant College of Beirut; of the work of Pilkington and Mackay in writing hymns for dark Uganda, of Pastor Coillard's hymns beloved in Sesuto, of Mrs. Marling's hymns among the savage Fan folk of the West Coast. From the multitudinous islands of the Pacific we should hear the songs which are the gifts of missionaries long since singing the songs of the redeemed in heaven. In the early days on blood-soaked Fiji, the little children were taught by Rev. John Watsford to sing the gospel stories of the life of Christ before they ever learned to read. The martyr, James Chalmers, insured the spread of the gospel for which he died, by translating into the language of the savage men of New Guinea nearly two hundred hymns.

Sales of hymn books The sales of hymn books have been only second to those of the Bible. The *Union Hymnal* published in Japan in 1903 contained hundreds of choice hymns, both original and translated, and became at once one of the best-selling books in Japan. These Christian hymns find their way into many non-Christian homes. They are adapted, words and all, for use in Buddhist Sunday schools.

"Buddha loves me, this I know,
For the Shastras tell me so."

Modern Buddhism creates no hymns; it patches up Christian hymns to suit its purposes.

Hymn writers; Indian

No sooner do Christian converts learn to sing the songs of Zion than they begin to express their new found faith in hymns of their own. An increasing number of these hymns is to be found in the hymnals of the rising churches of the Orient. In India, for example, rhyming paraphrases of Bible stories and teachings are set to Indian tunes and chanted to enraptured audiences. An audience of Telugu farmers will listen half the night to the life of Joseph or of Paul expressed in primitive verse-form and set to one of the well-known chants in which they have been wont to hear the traditions of their race. An increasing use is being made of this form for securing the entrance and lodgment of Christian truth. Many Indian pastors and evangelists are proving to have a great gift in thus singing the gospel into the hearts of the people. Several hymns written by Indian Christians have found their way into our American hymnal. Notable among these is *In the Secret of His Presence* by Ellen Lakshmi Goveh, a high-caste Hindu girl, and *O Thou my Soul, Forget no More* by Krishna Pal, the first Indian convert baptized by William Carey.

A notable hymn writer and evangelist

There died recently Mr. N. V. Tilak of Ahmednagar, India, a notable Christian, a man of rare poetic gifts whose hymns have entered into the imperishable treasury of the Marathi tongue. In his last will and testament he made confession of his Christian faith: "None knows when he will have the call of God," he writes, "and none ought to be thinking of it unnecessarily. That experience I am never willing to call Death. It is the call of God. It is awakening into a new life. The thought of it never disheartened me. No trouble while dying, no trouble while living, is the privilege of a Christian, and through Christ I enjoy it."

Quality of his hymns

Mr. Tilak's hymns are full of the noble rhythm and sonorous cadences of the Marathi language. They are mystical, full of poetry, and breathe a passionate devotion to Jesus. Through his hymns Mr. Tilak has become a beloved leader among Marathi Christians everywhere.

Much remaining to be done While it is encouraging to study what has been the effect of the introduction of the Bible in stimulating other forms of Christian literature it must not be forgotten that only a tiny beginning has been made. The call for the supply, and the distribution of Christian literature is just beginning to be heard as one of the outstanding needs of the lands now awaking to new life under the impact of the gospel. Neither in quantity, in quality; nor in subject matter is the literature now available satisfactory or sufficient.

Literature for the home Take for example the needs of the home. Two-thirds of the women of the world long denied education or books are beginning to go to school. Thousands of them are becoming literate each year. In most mission fields there is little except the Bible for them to read. In all but two or three fields there is a dearth of books regarding the care of children, the work of home building, Christian biography, fiction, books of devotion. The eloquent fact that in all China there is but one picture book for children makes a louder appeal for wholesome, homely, helpful books for the mother and the children than would pages of argument.

***A* Child's Life of Jesus** The strength of the appeal was shown recently when Mrs. MacGillivray of Shanghai was speaking about the need of children's books to an audience in Boston. She had described her visit to a book store in Toronto during holiday season with its bewildering array of children's books, stories, nature books, fairy tales, poems, travel, Bible stories, books about science, books showing how to weave baskets, do carpentry, raise bees, make gardens, take care of pets, make candy and all sorts of delightful things. Then she thought how a Chinese mother would have no trouble at all in deciding which picture book to take, because there would be only one. When she had finished speaking she was asked what book she would choose above all others to make for Chinese children. Without hesitation she said a *Child's Life of Jesus, Illustrated*. As soon as the meeting was over a lady hastened forward with her checkbook in hand, "It isn't necessary to pay for it now," said Mrs. MacGillivray, "it will take several months to secure the Chinese writer and an artist who will draw the pictures." "I might die on the way home," insisted the lady, "and I want the privilege of publishing that life of Jesus for little children." The three hundred and fifty dollars which she paid compensated writer and artist and paid for a first edition one thousand copies. The sale of the first edition will provide funds to issue the second edition.

Jubilee books

This idea of providing books for children has been taken up by the Woman's American Baptist Foreign Mission Society as part of its jubilee celebration. A fund has been set aside with which to publish one book or more in each of its fields. Wherever there is no *Child's Life of Jesus* the question of providing one will be taken up.

***Popularity of* Happy Childhood**

Encouragement is to be found in the response already made to this attempt to create a reading public among the young people. Mrs. MacGillivray reports that the little magazine *Happy Childhood* is eagerly looked for in every part of the world where there are Chinese people. The magazine was taken, for example, in a girl's school in Shansi. One number contained an account of a school for the deaf in Chefoo. This so interested the girls that they gave $3.00 (no small sum from their meager funds) and sent it to the school for the deaf. In far away Vancouver a little Chinese girl read the story that *Happy Childhood* brought the of the Door of Hope in Shanghai. She promptly began to tell other children about the Door of Hope and to interest them. They organized a little sewing society and made several warm quilts which they sent at Christmas to the Door of Hope and to a Chinese hospital.

Happy Childhood *in the palace*

Mrs. MacGillivray told another charming story about the little magazine. It seems that a missionary who was teaching the children of Yuan Shi Kai, the president of China, took a copy of *Happy Childhood* with her one day on her visit to the palace. Several times it happened that she left a copy. One day one of the secondary wives in the palace called her aside and said, "Tell me about this Jesus of whom this paper speaks so often." As she told her of Jesus, the old scene was repeated when "they of Caesar's household" listened to the apostle who brought them the good news.

Importance of periodicals

Considerations like the above reveal the necessity of fostering periodical literature, not too bookish and intellectual, for women and children. The women's boards have made a tiny beginning to supply this need through the publication of several women's magazines. Few, if any, of them have made library grants to assure that the magazines for women and children shall be taken in the schools and provided freely in reading rooms. No better reward of diligence could be given than to make a pupil a subscriber for a good Christian magazine.

Need of cooperation The business of publishing a magazine is expensive. A poor, shabby, dull paper defeats its ends. A wide-awake, spiritually stimulating child's paper has almost superhuman powers for good. The beginning of cooperation in which several boards unite in the support of one magazine has already been seen in China in the publication of *Happy Childhood.*

Call for adequate program The dearth of reading matter, the eager response with which our first limited attempts to supply the need are met, the absolute necessity of cultivating the reading habit if a vigorous, broad-minded Christian community is to be developed, all point to the need of an adequate program of advance. All the great missionary societies are planning for advance. Old programs and standards are being discarded as outgrown and insufficient. It is necessary that the lack of books be taken into account. There are few signs that this problem is being faced in any but the most desultory way. Here and there a board makes a grant. Now and then a missionary is set aside for literary work; but up to the present day no well-considered plan has been formulated and adopted for the whole field.

The program expensive Such a program means a large, a very large investment of money. If the people are too poor to buy books we must supply them; if they are too ignorant to desire books we must create the appetite. No self-supporting, self-propagating Protestant church can be created and maintained without books. The strong Protestant nations are all reading nations. The strong Protestant denominations are all reading denominations. We are people of the Book, of many books. Having begun our missionary campaign, we must carry it through. More books, and better, are a prime necessity. Until the awakening peoples can create a sufficient literature for themselves they must receive translations and adaptations of the most valiant and beautiful books that men have made. The torch which Greece and Rome and Israel passed on to Europe, and Europe in turn to America, must be passed to the Orient.

Outstanding opportunities (1) Publicity In formulating the enlarged program for the new day there are to be considered at least two tremendous opportunities. The one has already been briefly alluded to—the opportunity to make non-Christian people acquainted with the main facts of the gospel through publicity in the daily press. The circulation of daily newspapers in the Orient is itself of comparatively recent development. To take advantage of it for promoting the kingdom on the lines so practically demonstrated by Mr. Pieters in Oita prefecture requires a very large outlay of money. A committee, after an exhaustive survey, estimated that adequate plans for newspaper publicity throughout the Japanese empire would necessitate an outlay of 500,000 annually for five years. If only Tokyo were taken as the organizing center a worthy, though incomplete, campaign could be undertaken for $1,000 annually. The report of this committee is fascinating reading. It may be obtained from the Interchurch World Movement under the title *Seven Years of Newspaper Evangelism in Japan.*

Value of Christian publicity

Such an undertaking, cooperatively financed by the great Protestant Boards of Foreign Missions, not only in Japan, but in China, India, and the Near East, would have enormous capacity for good. It is not fanciful to dream such dreams in these days of wide open opportunity.

(2) Use of phonetic Chinese script

The second line of advance providentially opened is through the use of the recently invented phonetic characters for the printing of Chinese. Through this invention China advances by one leap from the position of the nation having a most archaic, cumbersome, and difficult system of writing the spoken word to that of the nation having a most advanced and scientific syllabary. Instead of a separate character to be memorized for each word in the language we have thirty-nine phonetic symbols based on the old characters. By means of certain diacritical marks placed above or beneath the characters it is possible to indicate the different tones. Such are the simplicity and beauty of the system that an illiterate adult can learn to read in a month or six weeks.

Advantage of phonetic system

It is difficult to overstate the importance of the new system of writing to the future progress of the Chinese people. The old character system of recording the language was acquired with difficulty by the common people and was but sketchily retained by many of them. The difficulty of reading books containing unfamiliar terms was enormous even to the educated. The problems of setting type or adapting the typewriter and other modern tools of business to Chinese were all but insuperable.

Overcoming Chinese conservatism

The conservatism of the Chinese and their deep pride in the literary beauties of their language have made all previous attempts to Romanize or to reform their ancient system of character writing abortive. The new system, because of its simplicity, its conformity to the traditional Chinese form, and the ease with which it is mastered, is rapidly growing in popularity. In Shansi, Governor Yen is enthusiastically pushing the new system in the hope of having the first literate province in China. Schools and colleges are falling in line, making the study of the new script a required topic. Students have been using their vacations for the purpose of teaching illiterates.

Printing of text-books

One of the first necessities in getting the new script studied is the preparation of textbooks. Fortunately the right person was already fitted for the task. Miss S. J. Garland of the China Inland Mission had for years been engaged in working out an improved system of braille for the use of the blind. Her system was generally recognized as the best, and her studies for the blind proved of service in working out the phonetic system of writing for the seeing. Her experience and reputation as a linguist led to her being asked to come to Shanghai and superintend the preparation of the first readers in the new script. Her board consented to release her. The first primer was already prepared when along came a truly staggering order from the governor of Shansi for 2.5 million primers. The order was divided among several printing firms in order to get it out in time. Other books are in process of preparation.

The Bible in the new script

The Gospels of Luke and Mark have already been translated from the Mandarin to the new phonetic characters. The American Bible Society has made a grant to cover the cost of printing. The use of the phonetic script makes it possible to put the Bible in the hands of the common people and quickly to teach them to read it for themselves. The diffusion of Christian truth thus made practicable may quicken the pace of China's evangelization by generations.

Importance of new script

The importance of this invention is yet but dimly realized. Not 40 million out of China's 400 million can read. The task of teaching them to read has been reduced from a matter of years to a matter of weeks. Such an emancipation as occurred with the rise of vernacular literature in Europe is bound to occur in China. The old classic writing and literature will never be displaced but will assume the place in a liberal education that the Latin and Greek classics have held in the Western world.

Opportunity of the church The church holds the key to this most wonderful door of opportunity. The Protestant church already has 125,000 literates to 188,000 illiterates. These reading Christians are for the first time able to teach their fellow villagers' to read and to place in their hands Christian teachings in this new everyday transcript of their everyday speech. This little army of literates is, for the most part, drawn from the common people, China's vast illiterate population. They are scattered through the villages. They are anxious to communicate the faith. What happened in Korea through the medium of Korea's easy phonetic script may happen in China; Christians may become people of the Book.

America's contribution During these days of the corruption and weakness of the Chinese government Christian America may work a mighty work for China and for the kingdom of God. It is in the power of American Christians to see that the first school books in the new script are Christian in background and viewpoint. We can rapidly put into phonetic characters the best Christian literature already available in Mandarin. We can provide and train a small army of teachers so that every Christian church shall become a recruiting station for the new learning. All this means money, but could money ever count for more? The Federation of Women's Boards has already responded, through its standing Committee on Christian Literature for Oriental Women and Children, by a small grant of $1,000. This must be followed up by grants from individual boards, by the setting apart of missionaries for this work, and by individual contributions in large amounts. What $100,000 wisely expended could do in assuring that the first contact with books should be Christian, it is difficult to overstate. The expenditure is not recurring. The art once taught will lift China from illiteracy to literacy. The people once reading will pay for their own books. China's age-long veneration for the printed page makes it particularly easy to use books in the interpretation of the Christian message, once the common people have access to books. The forces of evil will not be slow to seize such an opening. It is safe to predict that within ten years the worst and most destructive books of America and Europe will be purchasable in the new script. It is for Christians to show equal enterprise in making available the life giving books of our Christian civilization.

In conclusion We have traveled as in an airplane over a wide stretching country. We have beheld the lofty Himalayas of the Bible lifting their stainless summits across the path of the centuries. From their heights we have seen what rivers of the water of life take their rise to run softly far below through blossoming orchards and green meadows! We have traced their course through arid deserts which they have made to yield harvests for the hunger of the world. Showers of blessing condensed upon the mountains have revived distant plains. We have seen people climbing the sides of the illimitable range of Scripture and as they climbed their faces have lightened and from the summits they have beheld the land that is very far off and the glory of God.

From our brief study we have risen strengthened and calm. It is humanity's book, this Book of God. In its hand there are treasures for all humankind; in its heart a living message from the living God. To follow its teachings, to extend its influence, to preach its gospel, to make known its Savior, crucified and risen again, is the deepest joy and the supreme privilege of the Christian. In the humble hope that this study, simple and inadequate as it is, may strengthen and deepen the faith of those who follow it, this little book is written. If it shall lead one person to devote himself whole-heartedly to make the Bible known to those who know it not the writer will be glad and grateful.

A Brief Reading List

Chapter One

Missions in the Plan of the Ages, Carver (Revell).
A Tour of the Missions, Strong (Griffith & Rowland Press). Chapters 15, 16, 17.
The Hebrew Bible and the Israelitish Nation. (Centennial Pamphlet, see book list, chapter 4.)
Winning the World for Christ, Lambuth (Revell, 1915). Lectures 1 and 2.
Christian Epoch Makers, Vedder (Griffith & Rowland Press, Philadelphia). Chapter 1, "The Philosophy of Christian Missions."
The Bible a Missionary Book, Horton (The Pilgrim Press, 1908). Chapters 3–6.

Chapter Two

How Europe Was Won for Christianity, Stubbs (Revell). Chapters 1, 2.
Bible Reading in the Early Church, Harnack (Putnam, 1912).
Outlines of Missionary History, Mason (Doran, 1912). Chapter 2.
Two Thousand Years of. Missions before Carey, Barnes (Christian Culture Press, Chicago, 1900). Chapters 1–3.
New Testament Studies in Missions, Beach (Student Volunteer Movement, 1900).
Winning the World for Christ, Lambuth (Revell). Lecture 6.

Christian Epoch Makers, Vedder (Griffith & Rowland Press). Chapter 2.
The Bible a Missionary Book, Horton (Pilgrim Press). Chapters 1, 2.
Christianity and Civilization, Church (Macmillan, 1914).

Chapter Three

The Bible in Many Lands, Harris (Carey Press, London).
The Book and Its Travels, Harris (Carey Press, London), for boys and girls.
The Conversion of India, Smith (Revell).
Missionary Programs and Incidents, Trull (Second Series). Pp. 117, 118, 124, 125, 130. Missionary Education Movement.
Romance of Missionary Heroism, Lambert (London, 1909). Chapter 14.
The Soul of India, Howells (London, 1913). Pp. 562–67.
How Europe Was Won for Christianity, Stubbs (Revell).
Islam, A Challenge to Faith, Zwemer. Pp. 164, 210, 215 (Student Volunteer Movement).
The Steep Ascent, Entwistle (Revell). Chapter 8.
The Influence of the Bible on Civilization, von Dobschiitz (Scribner, 1914). Chapters 3, 6, and illustrations of early translations of the Bible.
The Story of the L. M. S., Horne (London; Simpkin, Marshall, & Co., 1904). Chapters 5, 7.
Two Thousand Years of Missions before Carey, Barnes. Illustrations of Nestorian Tablet, p. 108.
Christian Epoch Makers, Vedder.
China Mission Year Book (1913) (Missionary Education Movement, New York).
Bible in the British Museum, article in *London Quarterly Review,* 1894, vol. 178, pp. 157–184.
Latin Translation of the Bible, article in *The Churchman,* 1891, vol. 16, pp. 90–98.
Theology of Civilization, Dale (Crowell, 1899).
Scotland's Influence on Civilization, L. J. Halsey (Pres. Bd. of Pub.).
History of European Morals, Lecky (London).

Chapter Four

The Christian Crusade for World Democracy, Taylor and Luccock (Methodist Book Concern).

The Story of the Bible Society, Canton (London, 1904).
All about Japan, Belle Brain (Revell). Pp. 159–81.
Bible Society Centenary Pamphlets. Ten pamphlets issued by the British and Foreign Bible Society, 1904, 146 Queen Victoria St., London, E.C. These pamphlets are valuable in Chapters 3–5.
A Children's History of the Bible Society, Canton (Murray, London).
Centennial Pamphlets (American Bible Society, 1916).
Single pamphlets, postpaid, 5 cents; in quantities of tenor more, 3 cents each. Order, American Bible Society, Astor Place, New York, N.Y.
In the Vulgar Tongue, Bible House, Queen Victoria St. (London, 1914).
The Modern Call of Missions, Dennis (Revell, 1913). Chapters 1–4.
The Cross in Japan, Hagin (Revell, 1914). Pp. 163–73
Missionary Review of the World, August, 1919. *The Bible and the World's Future,* Mason.
The World Outlook, March, 1918, *The World's Best Seller.*

Chapter Five

The New Horoscope of Missions, Dennis (Revell). Lectures 2 and 3.
Ministers of Mercy, Franklin (Missionary Education Movement).
Epoch Makers of Modern Missions, McLean (Revell).
Missionary Programs and Incidents (Second Series), Trull (Missionary Education Movement).
African Missionary Heroes and Heroines, Kimm (Macmillan, 1917). Fine Maps.
The Story of the American Board, Strong (The Pilgrim Press). Pp. 272, 381.
Korea for Christ, Davis (London, 22 Paternoster Row, E.C.). P. 39.
Daybreak in the Dark Continent, Naylor (Missionary Education Movement). Pp. 223–33.
Human Progress through Missions, Barton (Revell, 1912).
Centennial Pamphlets, see book list, Chapter 4.
Evolution of the Use of the Bible in Europe, Kuyper.
The Bible, the Book of Mankind, Warfield.
Lincoln's Use of the Bible, Jackson (Abingdon Press).
The Bible and Civilization, von Dobschütz (Scribner). Chapters 4, 5.
World Facts and America's Responsibility, Patton (Association Press, 1919). Chapters 1–3.

Gesta Christi, Brace (Armstrong, 1903).
The Christian Movement in Japan (1814). Pp. 164–71. (Missionary Education Movement, New York.)
India's Silent Revolution, Fisher (Macmillan, 1919). Chapters 4, 6.
The Greatest English Classic, McAfee (Harper, 1912). Chapters 5, 6.
Is the World Growing Better? Snowdon (Macmillan, 1919). Chapter 9, "The Bible and Progress."
Civilization of Christendom, Bosanquet (Macmillan).
Influence of Christianity upon Social and Political Ideas (Milwaukee, Young Churchman, 1912).
Christianity and Civilization, Church (Macmillan, 1914).
Christ or Chaos, Watson (Pilgrim Press).

Chapter Six

Korea for Christ, Davis (London, 22 Paternoster Row, E.C.). See Chapter 9, "Whang, the Blind Sorcerer."
The Bible and Civilization, von Dobschiitz (Scribners). Chapter 7.
Christian Movement in Japan (Missionary Education Movement, New York).
See Volumes from 1914–1919 for Annual Review of Christian Literature.
See 1917, part 9, for Women's Movement, Industrial Conditions, Social Evil, Labor Movement.
See 1913, Chapter 30 on Newspaper Evangelism.
The Modern Call of Missions, Dennis (Revell, 1913). Chapter 10, "The Hymnody of Modern Missions."
Contrasts in Social Progress, Tenney (Rumford Press, Concord, N.H., 1914).
China Mission Year Book (1913) (Missionary Education Movement, New York). Pp. 308–13, 352–61.
T'he Literary Primacy of the Bible, Eckman (Methodist Book Concern, 1915). Chapters 1 and 4.
The Greatest English Classic, McAfee (Harper, 1912). Chapter 4.
Christian Literature in the Mission Field, Ritson (Edinborough, 1 Charlotte Square, 1910).
Worldwide Sunday-school Work. Report of Zurich Convention, 1913 (Pub. World Sunday-school Association, Metropolitan Tower, N.Y.).
Seven Years of Newspaper Evangelism in Japan, by Albertus Pieters, Oita, Japan.

Index